Green Finance and Investment

Mobilising Bond Markets for a Low-Carbon Transition

OECD
BETTER POLICIES FOR BETTER LIVES

This work is published under the responsibility of the Secretary-General of the OECD. The opinions expressed and arguments employed herein do not necessarily reflect the official views of OECD member countries.

This document and any map included herein are without prejudice to the status of or sovereignty over any territory, to the delimitation of international frontiers and boundaries and to the name of any territory, city or area.

Please cite this publication as:
OECD (2017), *Mobilising Bond Markets for a Low-Carbon Transition*, Green Finance and Investment, OECD Publishing, Paris.
http://dx.doi.org/10.1787/9789264272323-en

ISBN 978-92-64-27231-6 (print)
ISBN 978-92-64-27232-3 (PDF)

Series: Green Finance and Investment
ISSN 2409-0336 (print)
ISSN 2409-0344 (online)

Photo credits: Cover © mika48/Shutterstock.com.

Corrigenda to OECD publications may be found on line at: *www.oecd.org/about/publishing/corrigenda.htm*.

Foreword

In the Paris Agreement adopted in December 2015 by the 21st Conference of the Parties to the United Nations Framework Convention on Climate (COP21), Parties agreed to hold the increase in the global average temperature to well below 2°C and pursue efforts to limit the temperature increase to 1.5°C above pre-industrial levels. Parties also agreed to make finance flows consistent with a pathway towards low greenhouse gas emissions and climate-resilient development.

Following the success of COP21, green finance activities in 2016 advanced significantly, and particularly the issuance of green bonds. The G20 Leaders' Statement at Hangzhou in September 2016 recognised this development by stating: "We believe efforts could be made to… provide clear strategic policy signals and frameworks, promote voluntary principles for green finance, support the development of local green bond markets and promote international collaboration to facilitate cross-border investment in green bonds".

This report describes the development of the green bond market as an innovative instrument for green finance and provide policy makers with a review of relevant policy actions to date and options to promote further green bond market development and growth. The report also provides, for the first time, a quantitative framework for understanding possible directions of bond market evolution and for analysing the potential contribution that the bond markets can make to a low-carbon transition.

As a preview to this report, the OECD published a *Policy Perspectives* brochure on green bonds jointly with Bloomberg Philanthropies in December 2015 during COP21. Elements of the report were released in two separate papers as contributions to the G20 Green Finance Study Group: "Green bonds: Country experiences, barriers and options" (OECD, International Capital Market Association, Climate Bonds Initiative and the Green Finance Committee of China Society for Finance and Banking), which was published in September 2016 alongside the G20 Green Finance Synthesis Report; and "A quantitative framework for analysing potential bond contributions in a low-carbon transition", which was launched in October 2016 at the 3rd Green Investment Financing Forum in Tokyo.

Acknowledgements

This report is an output of the OECD Environment Directorate, directed by Simon Upton, and the subsidiary Climate, Biodiversity and Water Division led by Simon Buckle. This report was written by Christopher Kaminker, under the supervision of Robert Youngman and Simon Buckle. The author would like to thank, in particular, Hideki Takada for his valuable research assistance and Robert Youngman (OECD) and Ma Jun (People's Bank of China and G20 Green Finance Study Group Co-Chair) for their guidance, comments and encouragement.

The OECD would like to thank Bloomberg Philanthropies for generous support for and substantive contributions to this project, with special thanks to Kevin Sheekey and Meridith Webster. A separate *Policy Perspectives* brochure on green bonds, which introduced key messages from this report, was produced jointly with Bloomberg Philanthropies and benefited from input and advice provided by Daniel Firger, Lenora Suki and Curtis Ravenel, who also co-hosted a joint OECD-Bloomberg side event at the OECD during COP21. Thanks are also due to Lee Cochran for her contributions to the OECD's outreach and communications for the project. The report benefited from insights gained from the OECD's Green Investment Financing Forums (in June 2014, May 2015 and October 2016), the Green Bond Quantitative Consultation hosted by Bloomberg during the BNEF Summit (April 2015) and the G20 Green Finance Study Group meetings of 2016. It also draws on broader work undertaken by the OECD on public policies for facilitating green long-term infrastructure investment, which is generously supported by voluntary contributions from the Japanese Ministry of Finance.

The OECD worked with Vivid Economics to develop a quantitative model that underpins the analysis exhibited in Chapter 3. Robin Smale led and co-ordinated the contribution from Vivid Economics, developed by Karim Aitchabane and advised by Samuel Fankhouser. Fabian Kesicki and Michael Waldron (International Energy Agency) co-ordinated the data and review process for the IEA's scenarios used in the construction of the quantitative model. Hideki Takada and Ma Jun provided specific input and review for the Japanese and Chinese markets, respectively. The report was informed by a review of the academic literature conducted by John Parsons, Michael Mehling and Joshua Hodge of the Massachusetts Institute of Technology (MIT). The author is grateful to this project team for their expert comments and review throughout the development of the report as well as to the project advisors for Chapter 3: Sean Kidney and Beate Sonerud (Climate Bonds Initiative); Mark Fulton (Energy Transition Advisors); Sean Flannery (Meister Consultants); and Daniel Firger, Lenora Suki, Ethan Zindler and Nathan Serota (Bloomberg).

The author would like to thank his colleagues at the OECD and IEA Secretariats who provided valuable comments and review to the report: Richard Baron, Greg Briner, Tyler Bryant, Simon Buckle, Serdar Celik, Jane Ellis, Mats Isaakson, Fabian Kesicki, André Laboul, Stephen Lumpkin, Iota Nassr, Joel Paula, Andrew Prag, Michael Waldron, Gert Wehinger and Simon Upton. He would also like to thank the following expert reviewers for their inputs, comments and guidance: Roberta Benedetti del Rio (Generation Investment Management), Murray Birt (Deutsche Bank), Gordon Clark (Oxford University), Christopher Flensborg (Skandinaviska Enskilda Banken), Branimir Gruic (Bank for International Settlements), Anadi Jauhari (Emerging Energy and Environment Investment Group), Eila Kreivi (European Investment Bank), Mark Lewis (Barclays), Jean-Marie Masse (International Finance Corporation), Kyung-Ah Park (Goldman Sachs), Nicholas Pfaff (International Capital Market Association), Heike Reichelt (World Bank) and Mike Wilkins (S&P).

This report and work benefited from review and comments provided by the OECD Working Party on Climate, Investment and Development and the Environment Policy Committee; the Committee on Financial Markets and the OECD/G20 Taskforce on Institutional Investors and Long-Term Financing. The OECD/G20 Taskforce comprises government delegates to the OECD Insurance and Private Pensions Committee (IPPC) and its Working Party on Private Pensions (WPPP), as well as the OECD Committee on Financial Markets (CMF), the International Organisation of Pension Supervisor (IOPS) and other G20 government delegates. This report and work also benefited from review and comments provided by the "Greening the Bond Markets" sub-group of the G20 Green Finance Study Group, co-chaired by the People's Bank of China and the Bank of England.

Table of contents

Tables

Figures

Boxes

Acronyms and abbreviations

2DS	2°C energy investment scenarios (International Energy Agency)
ABS	Asset-backed security
ADB	Asian Development Bank
AuM	Assets under management
BNEF	Bloomberg New Energy Finance
BPS	Basis points (1/100th of 1%)
CBI	Climate Bonds Initiative
CLO	Collateralised loan obligation
CO_2	Carbon dioxide
COP	Conference of the Parties
EDF	Électricité de France
EIB	European Investment Bank
ESG	Environment, social and governance
GBP	Green Bond Principles
GEPF	Government Employees Pension Fund (South Africa)
GFC	Green Finance Committee
GFSG	Green Finance Study Group
ICMA	International Capital Market Association
IEA	International Energy Agency
IFC	International Finance Corporation
IFI	International financial institution
LCBM	Local currency bond market
LCR	Low-carbon and climate-resilient
LEV	Low-emission vehicle
MBS	Mortgage-backed securities
MW	Megawatt
NREL	National Renewable Energy Laboratory
OPIC	Overseas Private Investment Corporation

PACE	Property Assessed Clean Energy (United States)
PBoC	People's Bank of China
PRI	Principles for Responsible Investment
PV	Photovoltaic
SAPC	Solar Access to Public Capital
SSA	Supranational, sub-sovereign and agency
STS	Simple, transparent and standardised
UNEP	United Nations Environment Programme
UNFCCC	United Nations Framework Convention on Climate Change
WACC	Weighted average cost of capital
WHEEL	Warehouse for Energy Efficiency Loans (United States)

Executive summary

The growing green bond market

In the Paris Agreement, Parties agreed to hold the increase in the global average temperature to well below 2°C and pursue efforts to limit the temperature increase to 1.5°C above pre-industrial levels, and to make finance flows consistent with a pathway towards low greenhouse gas emissions and climate-resilient development. Recent estimates suggest that approximately USD 93 trillion in infrastructure investment will be needed in the next 15 years in a "low-carbon" scenario.

Debt currently finances the majority of infrastructure investment. In particular, bond finance is a natural fit for low-carbon and climate-resilient infrastructure assets such as renewable energy infrastructure, which is characterised by high upfront capital costs and long-dated and frequently inflation-linked income streams.

Since 2007-08 a market for bonds specifically "labelled" or designated as "green" ("green bonds") has emerged. A green bond is differentiated from a regular bond by its commitment to use the funds raised to finance or refinance "green" projects, assets or business activities. With growing market appetite for such bonds, annual issuance of labelled "green bonds" rose from just USD 3 billion in 2011 to USD 95 billion in 2016.

There are a number of international and national taxonomies addressing green bond project definitions, including the Green Bond Principles and the Climate Bonds Standard. However, the lack of universal rules and standardisation is a shared and enduring source of concern cited by participants in the market. Convergence towards commonly accepted definitions will be essential to maximise the effectiveness, efficiency and integrity of the market. At the same time, striking a balance between securing market confidence and reducing green transaction costs will be critical.

Green bonds can offer several important benefits for green investment including: 1) providing an additional source of green financing; 2) enabling more long-term green financing by addressing maturity mismatches; 3) enhancing issuers' reputation and clarifying environmental strategy; 4) offering potential cost advantages; 5) facilitating the "greening" of traditionally brown sectors; and 6) making new green financial products available to responsible and long-term investors.

Barriers, policy actions and options for green bond market development and growth

The evolving green bond market faces a range of specific challenges and barriers including: 1) general challenges to bond market development; 2) lack of awareness of the benefits of green bonds and existing international guidelines and standards; 3) lack of local green bond guidelines; 4) costs of meeting green bond requirements; 5) lack of green bond ratings, indices and listings; 6) lack of supply of labelled green bonds;

7) difficulties for international investors to access local markets; and 8) lack of domestic green investors.

There are various options and policy considerations for addressing these barriers that are already being used by the official sector in different jurisdictions globally:

- establishing enabling, "investment-grade" policy environment as preconditions
- careful design and calibration of regulatory frameworks
- market building, such as identifying project pipelines and developing green guidelines and standards; in particular, defining international rules could help overcome many of the barriers identified
- demand-side measures, such as giving public institutions mandates for green bond investment
- supply-side measures, such as public sector demonstration issuance and reducing costs of green bond issuance and reporting
- public intervention, such as risk mitigation.

A quantitative framework for analysing potential bond contributions in a low-carbon transition

This report proposes a framework for understanding possible directions of bond market evolution and for analysing the potential contribution that the bond markets can make to a low-carbon transition. The analysis studies: 1) how much debt finance is needed to meet the IEA's 2°C energy investment scenarios (2DS) between 2015 and 2035 in the four markets studied (the People's Republic of China, the European Union, Japan and the United States); 2) how the bond market might evolve in the same period to account for part of these debt finance needs; and 3) the implications for institutional investors that have driven the growth of the green bond market to date.

This analysis focuses on bond financing for the renewable energy, energy efficiency and low-emission vehicle sectors which account for 80-90% of the low-carbon assets included in the 2DS. Two main scenarios were modelled on a 2DS pathway: 1) a base-case scenario that uses conservative asset securitisation assumptions; and 2) a scenario with a 10% increase in asset securitisation rate across all sectors. Both main scenarios assume that policy makers adopt supportive policies to overcome various challenges.

The results of the analysis suggest that by 2035 in a 2DS, bonds financing and refinancing the three sectors in the four markets studied have the potential to scale to USD 4.7-5.6 trillion in outstanding securities globally and USD 620-720 billion in annual issuance. While these figures may seem large on an absolute basis, they are small (approximately 4%) relative to the scale of debt securities markets, generally with USD 19 trillion of gross issuance in the four markets in 2014.

The 2020s have the potential to be the start of the "golden years" for bond issuance in the low-carbon sectors. As low-carbon technologies mature and become more familiar to bond markets, and as the risks of assets fall as policy stabilises, the role played by bonds could expand rapidly. This analysis examines the potential for different types of bond to finance a range of sectors and sub-sectors of low-carbon investments studied. It displays a picture of the volume of outstanding securities through to 2035 and the speed at which they could potentially scale up.

Bond finance has the potential to play a significant role in mobilising additional institutional investors to support the low-carbon investment necessary to meet a 2DS by mid-century. Institutional investors in the OECD have the potential to absorb the increased supply of such bonds, through shifting asset allocations in response to the increased percentage of low-carbon bonds as a share of the broader bond markets. This conclusion is based on two assumptions: 1) institutional investors' appetite for low-carbon bonds may be expected to grow in light of increasing attention to climate risks and opportunities in investment portfolios; and 2) institutional investors will shift allocations to reflect the increasing share of low-carbon bonds in the market as a whole.

Chapter 1.

Mobilising bond markets for a low-carbon transition

This chapter describes the emergence of a market for green bonds, in the context of broader efforts to finance a low-carbon transition, and examines how the market has evolved. It describes the roles of a range of actors in the market, the continuing evolution of green bond definitions and governance standards. It also provides an overview of the advantages and disadvantages of green bonds as perceived by investors and issuers. This information provides the necessary introduction and context for the chapters that follow on barriers to market growth and actions that policy makers are taking to overcome them (Chapter 2), and a quantitative assessment of the role of bonds in a low-carbon transition (Chapter 3).

Raising the capital to finance a low-carbon transition

Climate change and the need to shift to low-carbon investment

In the Paris Agreement adopted in December 2015 by the 21st Conference of the Parties to the United Nations Framework Convention on Climate (COP21), Parties agreed to hold the increase in the global average temperature to well below 2°C and pursue efforts to limit the temperature increase to 1.5°C above pre-industrial levels. Parties also agreed to make finance flows consistent with a pathway towards low greenhouse gas emissions and climate-resilient development (UNFCCC, 2015).

Low-carbon energy sources are becoming more cost-competitive every month and deployment is rapidly scaling up. The International Energy Agency's (IEA) *Medium-Term Renewable Energy Market Report 2016* shows that in 2015, for the first time, renewables accounted for more than half of net annual additions to power capacity and overtook coal in terms of cumulative installed capacity in the world. Record deployment was accompanied by continued sharp reductions in generation costs, with announced long-term remuneration prices ranging from USD 30/megawatt hours (MWh) to 50/MWh for both onshore wind and solar (photovoltaic, PV) plants. Onshore wind generation costs are expected to decrease by a further 15% on average by 2021, while utility-scale solar PV costs are anticipated to decline by another quarter (IEA, 2016).

These trends are underpinned by a combination of sustained policy support, technology progress and expansion into newer markets with better renewable resources. The IEA projects that renewables are set to become the leading source of new energy supply from now to 2040 (IEA, 2015).

Investment needs and incremental costs of "going low carbon"

Global energy infrastructure needs and the increasingly pressing challenges and risks associated with climate change present the world with an unprecedented investment opportunity related to the transition to a low-carbon climate-resilient (LCR) economy. Recent estimates suggest that approximately USD 89 trillion in infrastructure investment across transport, energy and water systems will be needed in the next 15 years – or USD 5.93 trillion annually, on average (NCE, 2015) – in a "high-carbon" scenario (Figure 1.1). This is significantly higher than the approximately USD 3 trillion invested in all types of infrastructure today (Bielenberg et al., 2016). However, the incremental costs of making infrastructure investments "low carbon" rather than "high carbon" are estimated by the NCE (2015) to be only 4.5% (i.e. USD 4 trillion over the next 15 years, or USD 0.27 trillion per year on average). Green infrastructure[1] typically involves higher upfront investments than traditional infrastructure, but comes with a wider set of returns and benefits.[2]

The challenge is to ensure that investment capital is reallocated from high-carbon to LCR options. Strategies for closing the financing gap need to consider: 1) a policy regime that establishes price incentives and policy coherence; and 2) the significant financial, regulatory and structural constraints faced by traditional sources of financing for green infrastructure – governments, corporate actors (e.g. utilities, project developers and others) and the banking sector.

The global financial crisis, and responses to it, led to a transformation of the financial landscape, with changes in behaviour by the banking sector in particular. Long-term financing by banks has declined as they derisk (deleverage) globally, although it is beginning to revitalise in some areas (Pooler, 2014). In the capital markets, a range of factors, including ambiguous macroeconomic prospects and declining forecasted returns for equity investments in publicly traded companies, have had adverse effects on demand for long-term equity capital (OECD, 2015). In addition to constraints in the banking sector, other traditional sources of finance such as corporate actors also face their own constraints (OECD, 2015).

Figure 1.1. **Upfront capital costs to meet global infrastructure demand, 2015-30**

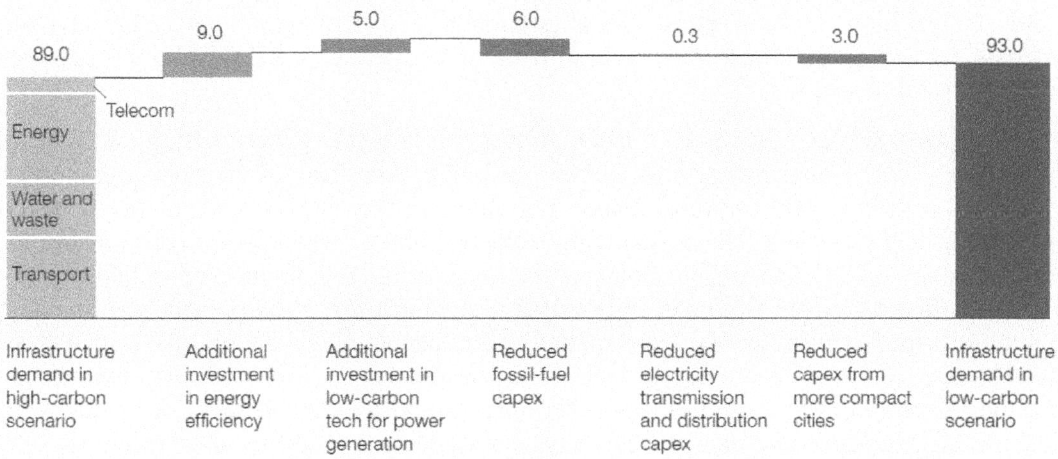

Note: Global demand for infrastructure services, USD trillion (constant USD 2010, indicative figures).

Source: NCE (2015), *Seizing the Global Opportunity: Partnerships for Better Growth and Better Climate*, http://newclimateeconomy.report/2015/wp-content/uploads/2014/08/NCE-2015_Seizing-the-Global-Opportunity_web.pdf.

Despite these constraints, the banking sector remains a key provider of investment financing, but it likely will not be able to compensate for constraints among other traditional sources and fill the massive financing gap for sustainable infrastructure on its own. For instance, the People's Bank of China (PBoC) estimates that the People's Republic of China (hereafter "China") will need to invest at least RMB 2 trillion (USD 320 billion) per year in green sectors in order to meet the environmental targets under the 13th Five Year Plan (2016-20). Public fiscal resources, however, can cover no more than 15% of these investments (PBoc/UNEP, 2015).

A related and broader issue is whether the financial system can enable capital reallocation consistent with the "green" transition and for the long run, i.e. by providing financing for companies and industries that protect and improve the environment and shifting financing away from fossil fuel industries and environmentally harmful activities (Boissinot, Hubert and Lame, 2016). It is only through such a reallocation that the infrastructural foundations of the global economy can be rewired to be consistent with keeping the global temperature increase to well below 2°C, as called for under the Paris Agreement.

The need to mobilise debt capital and bonds

While the scale of investment needs is relatively well known, policy makers need a clearer understanding of whether investment needs could feasibly be financed from private sources of debt and equity capital, and if so, how this might be done. Debt currently finances the majority of infrastructure investment but the challenge will be to shift this debt investment away from emissions-intensive investments while scaling up investment in LCR infrastructure.

The typical debt-to-equity ratio in overall infrastructure project finance is 70:30 (Dobbs et al., 2013), with either the same ratio of debt in renewable energy financing as estimated by Zindler and Locklin (2016), or a somewhat higher proportion of debt as estimated by McKinsey (75:25). The ratio is approximately 50:50 for financing energy efficiency and low-emissions vehicles.[3] According to the Zindler and Locklin (2016), in 2015 a record USD 266 billion was invested in new renewable power generation (with USD 200 billion in new build asset financing, and the remainder split between refinancing and acquisitions of assets), up from an average of USD 250 billion per year over the last four years.

As illustrated in Figure 1.2, through analysis of the Bloomberg New Energy Finance's (BNEF) database, debt accounted for USD 186 billion of the financing amount in 2015, with the vast majority being provided in the form of loans by financial institutions and on-balance sheet financing from corporates, which is also responsible for half of equity investment. While bonds were used to directly finance or refinance only USD 6 billion out of the USD 266 billion in investment in 2015, corporates and financial institutions routinely call on the bond market to fund and refinance their on-balance sheet investment,; although this practice varies geographically. Financial institutions, for instance, rely to a large extent on bonds to raise capital for their lending activities, with US and EU commercial banks currently maintaining a bond-to-loan ratio of 30% (Bielenberg et al., 2016; ECB, 2015).

Figure 1.2. **Investment in renewable energy in 2015 and the role of bonds**

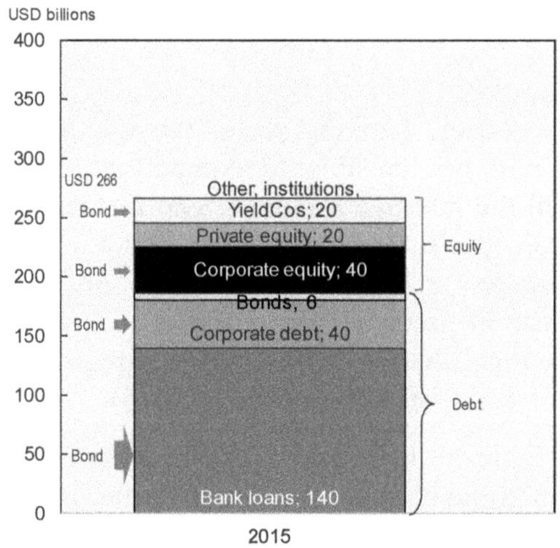

Note: In 2015 YieldCos used bonds to fund wind farm acquisitions and a private equity fund used a bond to refinance a portfolio of wind farms. "Other" includes institutional investors and other non-bank intermediaries. Bond arrows are not drawn to scale and are provided to illustrate that they are used to raise funding for varying portions of the investment activity.

Source: OECD analysis based on the *BNEF database*.

In 2014 the total amount of capital held in global debt securities (i.e. bonds, notes and money market instruments) markets issued by all types of entities (banks, governments, corporations, etc.) was estimated at USD 97.2 trillion (Figure 1.3). The broader debt capital markets include a further USD 66 trillion in loans outstanding in 2010 (the most recent estimate available) (Roxburgh, Lund and Piotrowski, 2011). Bond[4] finance is a natural fit for LCR infrastructure assets. The case is especially clear for renewable energy infrastructure, which is characterised by high upfront capital costs and long-dated and frequently inflation-linked income streams. Many cities and municipalities rely on bonds to raise the financing for their low-carbon development plans.

Figure 1.3. **USD 97 trillion of outstanding global debt securities in 2014**

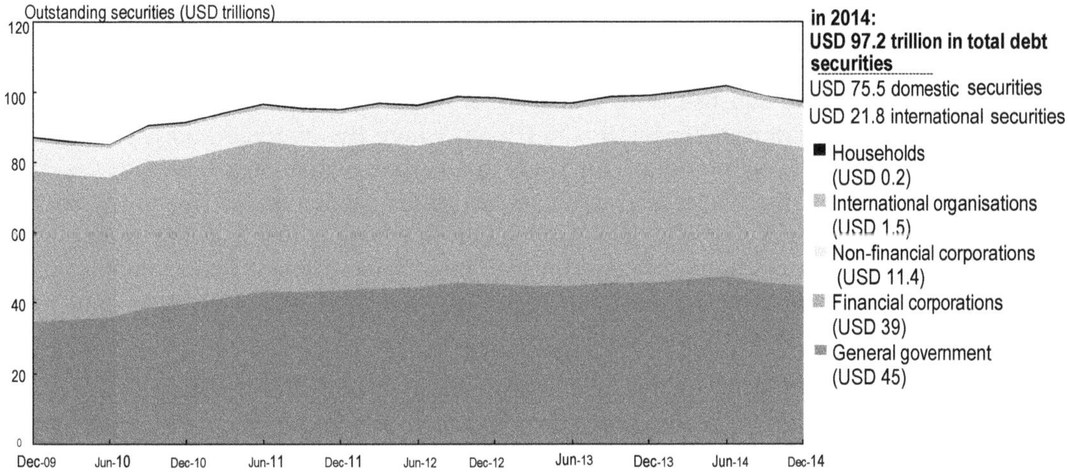

Note: Debt securities include a variety of instruments such as bonds, notes and money market instruments, which have different maturities and intended purposes, most of which are not related to infrastructure finance. There is potential overlap between domestic and international securities.

Source: OECD analysis based on BIS debt securities statistics.

Banks and corporates will continue to be an important source of direct LCR infrastructure finance, especially at earlier stages of project finance. However, the scale of investment needs along with the "maturity mismatch" (short-term funding of long-term assets) in asset financing significantly exceeds the capabilities of a post-financial crisis banking sector and an electric utility sector with increasingly constrained balance sheets (Buehler, Noteboom and Williams, 2013; Alvarez et al., 2013; Gerken et al., 2013). Bond markets, which provide a funding source and an alternative to bank and corporate financing, will need to play a pivotal role.

Given that the cost of project finance debt arranged by banks is higher than the yield for investment-grade project bonds in most jurisdictions,[5] it may be possible to achieve a reduction in the weighted average cost of capital (WACC) for LCR infrastructure financed or refinanced with bonds (WEF, 2013), although the cost of capital is usually an inherent feature of the project and its risk, which can have more impact than the financing method used.

Bonds can raise capital directly for LCR projects, or they can refinance existing shorter term loans potentially at a lower cost. For instance, in 2015, the Blackstone Group refinanced loans to build German offshore wind parks by selling USD 1 billion of green bonds to investors who were prepared to accept a lower interest rate for the investment-grade bonds than Blackstone agreed to pay to nine lenders at an earlier stage in the project's development, when risks were higher. Lowering the cost of capital for renewable energy is important because an estimated 50-70% of the costs of electricity generation are in the financial cost of capital, with only the balance being the physical or operational costs of the installation (OECD, 2015). Thus, even small changes in the

WACC can have substantial impact on the long-term levelised cost of capital-intensive renewable energy projects and their competitiveness.

A bond market provides greater flexibility and more options for early project phase capital to be freed up after it has been deployed (an "exit"), as well as for the longer term project finance debt held by banks constrained by deleveraging and regulations. In this way, bonds can help to increase the speed at which capital can be "recycled" back into development, construction and early-stage risk, and also help to attract additional early-stage finance. Investors are more likely to invest their capital in construction if there is a credible and predictable low-cost exit once assets become operational (Caldecott, 2012).

Financial institutions can use bonds to resolve maturity mismatches between loans and liabilities. This is a particular priority in China, where the average liability maturity in the banking industry is six months. This leads to a maturity mismatch with the need for green infrastructure lending where average loan maturities needed are of five to ten years. To address this issue and promote increased green lending in the banking sector, the PBoC established a green bond system for the inter-bank market which enables the issuance of green bonds with longer maturities (see Box 1.6), that also help banks to hedge "duration risk" (PBoC/UNEP, 2015).

Bonds also provide the advantage of already being a well-established asset class in the investment portfolios of mainstream institutional investors that have significant potential to finance a low-carbon transition as analysed by the OECD (OECD, 2015; Kaminker and Stewart, 2012). Institutional investors in the OECD managed USD 93 trillion of assets in 2014, with bonds being the asset class favoured by OECD pension funds and insurance companies, allocating 53% and 64% respectively of their portfolio to bonds in 2013 (simple average).[6] Bonds with longer maturities are potentially a good fit with institutional investors' long-term liabilities, allowing for asset-liability matching. Green bonds in particular can reconcile the emerging demand (Box 1.3) from institutional investors for sustainability-themed and environment, social and governance (ESG)-screened investments with infrastructure investment needs.

The green bond market

What is a green bond?

As shown in the previous section, the use of bonds to finance large-scale LCR infrastructure directly or to fund lending is not new. However, since 2007-08 a market for bonds specifically "labelled" or designated as "green" (hereafter "green bonds") has emerged. The green bond market emerged with the first few issuances by multilateral development banks. From 2007-12, the market mainly featured issuance of green bonds by so-called supranational, sub-sovereign and agency (SSA) actors such as the European Investment Bank (EIB), the International Finance Corporation (IFC) and the World Bank, along with a few local government funding agencies, municipalities and national development banks.

With growing market appetite for such bonds (described in Box 1.3), the range of issuers and investors participating in the green bond market expanded significantly with corporates and banks entering the market in 2013. Annual issuance of labelled "green bonds" rose from just USD 3 billion in 2011 to USD 48 billion in 2015, with issuance occurring in 14 of the G20 markets. Annual green bond issuance continued to grow rapidly in 2016 bolstered by the entrance of Chinese issuers in the market, with USD 95 billion[7] issued. Figure 1.4 illustrates the composition of green bond issuance through to 2016.

Box 1.1. Defining a green bond

Green bonds are debt instruments used to finance green projects that deliver environmental benefits. A green bond is differentiated from a regular bond by its commitment to use the funds raised to finance or refinance "green" projects, assets or business activities. Green bonds can be issued by either public or private actors up front to raise capital for projects or for refinancing purposes, freeing up capital and leading to increased lending. (OECD et al., 2016)

Green bond project definitions and requirements for disclosure of the use of proceeds are the basis for developing a credible green bond market by avoiding "green washing". Globally, the most widely accepted standards are the Green Bond Principles (GBP), a set of voluntary guidelines elaborated by key market participants under the co-ordination of the International Capital Market Association (ICMA), and the Climate Bonds Standard, which also includes sector-specific criteria, developed by "scientific experts under the stewardship of the Climate Bonds Initiative (CBI)". The GBP define green bonds as "any type of bond instrument where the [issuance] proceeds will be exclusively applied to finance or re-finance in part or in full new and/or existing eligible Green Projects" and "which are aligned with the four core components of the GBP" (ICMA, 2016).[1]

While the OECD has not defined what constitutes a green investment, it has discussed it in its working definitions for "green infrastructure" and for "green investments" (OECD, 2013; Inderst et al., 2012) and has provided a general quantitative basis for assessing to what extent infrastructure systems can be considered "low-carbon and climate-resilient" (Kennedy and Corfee-Morlot, 2012). In terms of coverage of green investment needs, this report's bond modelling scenarios in Chapter 3 are limited to the renewable energy, energy efficiency and low-emissions vehicle sectors as estimated by the IEA (2014) to be consistent with a 2°C emissions path.

Note: 1. The GBP have four core components: 1) use of proceeds; 2) process for project evaluation and selection; 3) management of proceeds; and 4) reporting (ICMA, 2016).

These green bonds are issued into a broader market of USD 694 billion in outstanding bonds,[8] comprising USD 576 billion of "unlabelled climate-aligned" bonds as designated by the NGO Climate Bonds Initiative (CBI), and USD 118 billion of labelled green bonds (CBI/HSBC, 2016). Unlabelled climate-aligned bonds are bonds whose proceeds are used to finance LCR industries and sectors but do not yet carry the green label (CBI/HSBC, 2015).[9] For instance, traditional bonds of "pure-play" wind energy companies qualify as unlabelled green bonds, as do rail bonds in China and France where the use of proceeds have been specified (note that rail bonds where proceeds are used for fossil fuel transport are excluded by the CBI). Most issuers of such bonds may not yet be aware of the potential utility of using the green label (as discussed in Table 1.4); and some issuers may choose not to label bonds as green due to concerns over a lack of standardisation in the market, political or stakeholder sensitivities, and concerns over restrictions associated with the label. Labelled green bonds issued globally in 2015 represented less than 1% of total US bond issuance alone and less than 0.2% of debt securities issued globally.

There are both narrow and broad definitions of green bonds. The narrow definition includes only "labelled" green bonds, including self-labelled and those labelled by independent reviewers. The broader definition also includes unlabelled "pure-play" bonds in sectors that are considered as "green" without controversies.[10] The broadest definition is the aforementioned "climate-aligned bonds" as defined by the CBI, which includes many unlabelled bonds that are assessed by the CBI to be "green".[11]

Figure 1.4. **Composition of the green bond market**

USD billion, gross issuance

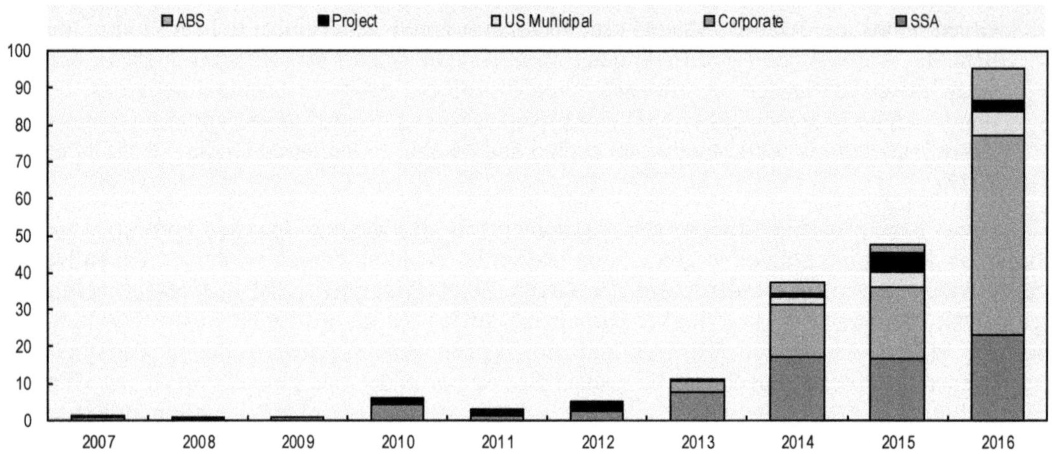

Note: "SSA" includes supranational, sub-sovereign and agency issuers such as development banks, local funding authorities, export credit agencies, etc. "Corporate" includes sectors such as utilities/energy, financials, consumer discretionary and staples, technology, industrials and others. This figure includes project bonds that are "tagged green" on the Bloomberg Terminal which are not included in other lists such as that of the Climate Bonds Initiative. Note also that 2016 figures include all Chinese green bonds issued in line with the People's Bank of China green catalogue, although some of these do not meet international investor expectations of green bonds due to the inclusion of "clean coal".

Source: SEB analysis provided to OECD, based on Bloomberg data.

Box 1.2. **Financial characteristics of green bonds**

Like any other bond, a green bond is a fixed-income financial instrument for raising capital from investors through the debt capital market. In line with mainstream bonds, the bond issuer raises a fixed amount of capital from investors over a set period of time (the "maturity"), repaying the capital (the "principal") when the bond matures and paying an agreed amount of interest ("coupons") along the way. They can be structured as asset-backed securities tied to specific green infrastructure projects, but to date have most commonly been issued in the form of "use-of-proceeds" bonds that raise capital to be allocated across a portfolio of green projects. A green label can also be applied to a bond by another entity via its inclusion in a green bond index (see Box 1.5) or via a "tag" on analytical tools widely used in financial markets, such as the Bloomberg Terminal.[1]

Note: 1. To tag a bond as "green", Bloomberg examines bond documentation and official statements for clear indication of an issuer's intention to both label a bond as green and clearly specify that the use of proceeds advances climate change mitigation or adaptation or promotes other environmental sustainability solutions.

As shown in Figure 1.5, in 2015, 46% of proceeds raised from green bond issuance were dedicated to financing renewable energy, followed by energy efficiency (20%), low-carbon transport (13%), sustainable water (9%), waste and pollution (6%), climate adaptation (4%), and agriculture and forestry (2%).

Figure 1.5. **Green bond use of proceeds raised in 2015 by sector**

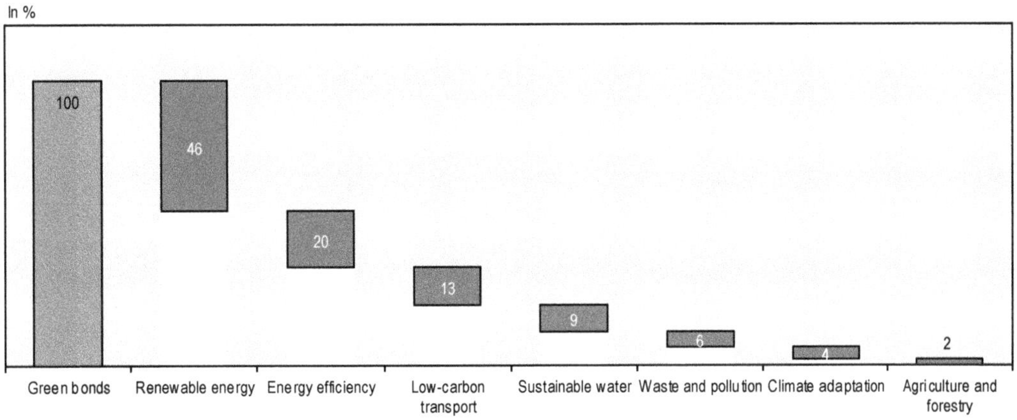

Source: OECD analysis based on CBI (2016), "Final year end green bond market roundup report", www.climatebonds.net/files/files/2015%20GB%20Market%20Roundup%2003A.pdf.

Promoting environmental integrity in the green bond market through guidelines and standards

The momentum of continued issuance and market demand has led to growing consensus on what constitutes a green bond and progress has been made on standards and criteria for what constitutes a green project or activity. The green bond market is underpinned by voluntary guidelines and standards, as well as more recently by rules and regulations in some jurisdictions such as China, France and India. Market and government-led efforts at standardisation and definition in the green bond market have borne fruit, with the emergence of the Green Bond Principles (GBP, a self-regulatory initiative designed to promote transparency and disclosure in the market).

Box 1.3. **Investor demand for sustainability and for green bonds rises**

Assets under management by signatories to the UN-supported Principles for Responsible Investment now stand at more than USD 60 trillion (according to the PRI), up from USD 4 trillion at the PRI's launch in 2006. So-called sustainably invested assets increased 61% globally in two years to USD 21.4 trillion at the start of 2014, with half of the assets allocated to bonds (Global Sustainable Investment Alliance, 2015). Socially responsible investors as well as mainstream investors that screen for environment, social and governance (ESG) factors have indicated their demand for green bonds. Pledges have been made to invest a defined amount into green bonds and investor statements supporting the growth of the green bonds market have been released.

In response to the greater availability of green bonds, a dozen institutional investors have made commitments or targets for green bond investments in excess of USD 15 billion to date, and 14 dedicated green bond funds have emerged (with 9 launched in 2015 alone). In 2016, the Swedish pension fund AP2 established a stand-alone green bond portfolio, arguing the market has "achieved a maturity and size" to justify the fund implementing a separate investment strategy and classifying its green bond holdings as a distinct asset class. In the margins of COP21, asset owners, investment managers and individual funds managing over USD 11.2 trillion of assets signed a statement in support of the green bond market. A 2014 investor statement on green bonds signed by investors with USD 2.6 trillion of assets under management was followed in 2015 with another investor statement setting out expectations for the green bond market (Ceres, 2015). The statement's 26 signatories pledged to carry out additional due diligence when evaluating bonds that finance projects whose environmental benefits are marginal. The statement also notes the expectation of annual impact reporting and the need for independent assurance or auditing of the selection and tracking of green projects.

Box 1.3. **Investor demand for sustainability and for green bonds rises** *(continued)*

Table 1.1. **Over EUR 12 billion in institutional commitments or targets for green bond investment, May 2016**

Green bond commitments or targets			
Actor	Sector	Commitment	Comments
Credit Agricole	Bank	EUR 2 billion	Target by end of 2017
Barclays	Bank	GBP 2 billion	Increased from GBP 1 billion target
KfW	Public financial institution	EUR 1 billion	Within four years
HSBC	Bank	USD 1 billion	No time frame
Zurich	Insurer	USD 2 billion	No time frame
Actiam	Asset manager	EUR 1 billion	No time frame
AXA	Insurer	EUR 1 billion	No time frame
Aviva	Insurer	Increase holdings	No time frame
Deutsche Bank	Bank	EUR 1 billion	No time frame
California State Treasury	Public financial institution	USD 1.1 billion	No time frame
Bangladesh Central Bank	Central bank	Some of its foreign currency reserves	No time frame
AP2	Pension fund	1% of portfolio allocation	No time frame
AP4	Pension fund	Strong commitment and significant allocation to green bonds	No time frame

Table 1.2. **Fourteen green bond funds manage EUR 1.16 billion, May 2016**

Actor	Focus	Assets under management
Storebrand	Green bond fund	EUR 500 million
Foresight	Unlabelled green bond fund	EUR 200 million
Humanis	Green bond fund ("HGA Obligations Vertes")	EUR 125 million
SEB	Green bond fund	EUR 110 million
AXA IM	Green bond fund (WF Planet Bonds)	EUR 80 million
Mirova	Green bond fund	EUR 62.55 million
Calvert	Green bond fund	EUR 61.29 million
Erste Asset Management	Responsible bond global impact fund	EUR 41.6 million
Raiffeisen Capital Management	Green bond fund	EUR 35 million
Allianz	Green bond fund	EUR 20 million
State Street	Green bond fund	EUR 20.34 million
Columbia Threadneedle	Social bond fund	USD 20 million
NN Investment Partners	Euro green bond fund	EUR 20 million
Nikko AM	World Bank green bond fund	SGD 16.46 million

The GBP, updated in June 2016, have achieved broad market acceptance as well as growing recognition by policy makers and regulators. As of June 2016, over 117 green bond issuers, underwriters and investors had become members of the GBP and in excess of 73 organisations were observers. The GBP outline voluntary guidelines for issuing green bonds, focusing on disclosure and transparency. They also provide guidance on eligible green project types through key areas of concern and the high-level project categories described below.

There are a number of international and national taxonomies addressing green bond project definitions, including the Climate Bonds Standard issued by the CBI and the Green Bond Endorsed Project Catalogue (2015 edition) issued by the Green Finance Committee (GFC) of the China Society for Finance and Banking. These and other principles and guidelines recognised and backed by the official sector – including public financial institutions and development banks – are discussed below.

However, as previously examined by the OECD (OECD, 2015; Inderst et al., 2012), the lack of universal rules and standardisation of green definitions, reporting and impact assessment is a shared and enduring source of concern cited by participants in the market. According to KPMG (2015), issuers face reputational risk and potential accusations of so-called "greenwashing" if proceeds are not used for their intended purposes or if issuers are unable to prove that proceeds have funded projects with positive and additional impact.

The risks of greenwashing are legitimate as over the past few years several green bond issuances have proven controversial among stakeholders. In 2015, an open letter signed by a coalition of 17 non-governmental organisations was submitted to the Green Bond Principles calling for them to better address transparency (Banktrack, 2015). The spectre of greenwashing has necessitated focused attention from market participants and stakeholders to safeguard the environmental integrity of the market, with the WWF in particular calling for "vigorous, credible, fully-developed and widely-accepted industry standards for green bonds being urgently needed to ensure that the market thrives and the sustainable economy grows" (WWF, 2016). At the same time, there are also concerns among market participants that attempts to establish stringent requirements and standards for bonds to qualify as "green" could slow, inhibit or derail the growth of a potentially critical source of capital for LCR infrastructure at an early stage of the market's development (Deutsche Bank, 2015; Wilkie, 2015; Gilbert, 2015).

Transparency in the "use of proceeds" as a key to integrity

In response to these tensions, a significant amount of effort has gone into shaping and cultivating a better-defined market with assurances for the environmental integrity and impact of green bonds while keeping "green transaction costs" low or seeking to drive them lower. Much of this work has involved determining what investments count as "green"; enhancing the transparency of the process by which a green bond is issued and how the proceeds are used and managed; and also on improving data and impact reporting.

The foundation of the green bond market lies in the utilisation of the proceeds of the bond which, according to the GBP, should be "appropriately described in the legal documentation for the security". The GBP recommend that "designated green project categories should provide clear environmentally sustainable benefits, which, where feasible, will be quantified or assessed by the issuer".

The GBP explicitly recognise several "broad categories" of potentially eligible green projects aiming to address key areas of concern such as climate change, natural resources depletion, biodiversity conservation and pollution.[12] The GBP do not currently define the type of projects under the general categories that qualify as "green", but point issuers and other stakeholders to existing, independently developed sets of criteria and standards for defining eligible green projects that can be used as a guide.

For instance, the Climate Bond Initiative's taxonomy (Table 1.3) specifies the green definitions for the Climate Bond Standards and Certification Scheme and is guided by a panel of climate and energy experts. It is the only current industry effort to address the challenge of green standards within each of the broader asset categories provided by the GBP. The CBI aims to encourage common definitions across global green bond markets based around its taxonomy. As of June 2016, 16 green bonds amounting to USD 6 billion in issuance and 15% of the green bonds issued in 2016 had been certified against the Climate Bonds Standard.

Table 1.3. **A taxonomy provides "green definitions" for Climate Bond Standards and Certification Scheme**

Energy	Transport	Water	Low-carbon buildings	Information technology and communications	Waste and pollution control	Nature based assets	Industry and energy-intensive commercial
Solar	Rail	Built (grey) infrastructure	Residential	Power management	Recycling	Agricultural land	Manufacturing
Wind	Vehicles	Green and hybrid infrastructure	Commercial	Broadband	Other recovery	Forests (managed and unmanaged)	Energy efficiency processes
Geothermal	Mass transit		Retrofit	Resource efficiency	Disposal	Wetlands	Energy efficiency products
Hydropower	Bus rapid transport		Products for building carbon efficiency	Tele-conferencing	Prevention	Degraded lands	Retail and wholesale
Bioenergy	Water-borne transport				Reuse	Other land uses (managed and unmanaged)	Data centres
Wave and tidal	Alternative fuel infrastructure				Pollution control	Fisheries and aquaculture	Process and fugitive emissions
Energy distribution and management						Coastal infrastructure	Energy-efficient appliances
Dedicated transmission						Land remediation	Combined heat and power

Source: Climate Bonds Initiative.

Review and assurance in the green bond market

A key element in the development of standards involves working out exactly how to verify the proper use of proceeds. While shortcomings in the disclosure of information about the use of proceeds may, for instance, be alleviated by the guidelines set out in the GBP, these are voluntary guidelines only, and do not currently spell out material requirements for the type and nature of activities, nor do they mandate a certain threshold of environmental benefits.

Investors need to be assured that the proceeds of the green bonds in which they invest are being allocated to appropriate qualifying projects that generate the desired "green" impacts. To secure this assurance in the absence of market-wide standardisation, the "majority of issuers" (CBI/HSBC, 2015) choose to retain specialist service providers and undergo independent review through assurance processes that include second-party reviews and consultation, audits and third-party certifications (Box 1.4). These different processes have been used on their own, or in combination, and serve to elucidate and validate the environmental criteria the issuer will use to select projects for funding, check compliance of the bonds against criteria specified by standards, and provide independent assurance about whether the bond's proceeds have been applied and managed as intended.

An ecosystem of green bond assurance providers has emerged to service this demand (Box 1.4).[14] These organisations verify the environmental integrity and impact of green bonds as well as the process by which a green bond is issued, managed and reported on. A number of private and academic organisations provide assurance on alignment with the GBP or on climate bonds certification, as well as on the eligibility of environmental projects. Some are also developing different types of green ratings. CICERO, a second-party reviewer of green bonds, offers a "Shades of Green" methodology whereby green bonds are graded "dark, medium or light" green depending on the underlying project's contribution to "implementing a 2050 climate solution" (Clapp and Torvanger, 2015). Industry-specific guidelines exist, such as those for real estate proposed by the Global Real Estate Sustainability Benchmark.

Box 1.4. Review and assurance in the green bond market

The Green Bond Principles (GBP) describe a variety of ways for issuers to obtain outside input to the formulation of their green bond process and recommend several levels and types of independent assurance.

Second-party reviews and consultation. For example, an issuer can seek advice from consultants and/or institutions ("second party") with recognised expertise in environmental sustainability to review or help in the establishment of its process for project evaluation and selection, including project categories eligible for green bond financing. The reviews and reports of the second party are private and may be made publicly available only at the discretion of the issuer.

Audits. Issuers are encouraged to have independently verified or audited certain aspects of their green bond process, such as the internal tracking method and the allocation of funds from proceeds. The verification can be provided by qualified third parties, or by internal and/or external auditors. These independent reports and audits may be put in the public domain at the discretion of the issuer.

Third-party certifications. Second-party standards intended for use by qualified third parties to certify green bonds are in use or in development. The GBP are supportive of the development of and use of such standards (e.g. the Climate Bonds Standard) for the certification of green bonds as they are defined above.

Ratings agencies are potential players for providing external reviews of green bonds. Certain rating agencies are exploring providing a rating of disclosure and transparency of green bonds. The international ratings agency Moody's launched a green bond rating methodology and service in 2016 – the first from a ratings agency. The Moody's Green Bond Assessment product is an evaluation focused on the issuer's adherence to best practice process – use of proceeds, management of proceeds and reporting rather than a direct evaluation of the relative level of green of assets and projects financed by the bond. For that aspect, Moody's scores a bond based on the green criteria resource that has been used to justify its green status, such as the GBP, the GFC or the CBI. S&P Global Ratings also proposed a new Green Bond Evaluation Tool to analyse and estimate the environmental impact of bond projects or initiatives.

Guidelines specific to municipal issuances have been developed, e.g. the Green Muni Bonds Playbook (Green City Bonds Coalition, 2015), as well as a framework developed by 11 international financial institutions active in the green bond market to harmonise impact indicators and reporting (ICMA, 2015). Several green bond benchmark indices have been launched to track performance and help formalise what qualifies as green by specifying specific attributes as requirements for inclusion in the index (Box 1.5).

Box 1.5. The emergence of green bond benchmark indices and exchange listings

As the green bond market has expanded and investor appetite increased, so too has the need for comparable performance data and the need to create benchmarks or reference points for performance. Market indices are broadly defined as metrics, often statistical, that track the performance of a specific group of securities or investment vehicles. In 2014 a range of banks, ratings agencies and service providers launched green bonds indices. These indices are aimed at lowering information barriers facing investors by providing clear risk-return data for this category of securities. Many institutional investors are required to invest exclusively in "benchmark-eligible" securities, so having a green bond included in a benchmark index can be an important attribute for attracting these mainstream investors. As of November 2016, five "families" of green bond indices were available to investors, each with different methodologies for calculation and with eligibility thresholds for green bonds (including currency, size, rating, and extra-financial characteristics like second-party opinions).

Indices also take a view on what projects and activities are eligible. For instance, to qualify for the Barclays MSCI Index, proceeds must be used for either new or existing environmental projects in five broad categories: alternative energy, energy efficiency, green building, pollution prevention and control, and sustainable water. Stock exchanges have built on these efforts and have launched dedicated green bond listings which provide added data and trading capabilities for market participants. As of 2016, green bonds were listed on stock exchanges of London, Luxembourg, Mexico, Oslo and Stockholm. The five indices and their green criteria are:

1. Bank of America Merrill Lynch Green Bond Index (complies with Bloomberg green bond definition)
2. Barclays MSCI Green Bond Index (complies with the Climate Bonds taxonomy and MSCI environmental assessment; unlabelled climate bonds are eligible)
3. S&P Green Bond Index (complies with the Climate Bonds taxonomy)
4. Solactive Green Bond Index (complies with the Climate Bonds taxonomy)
5. ChinaBond China Climate-Aligned Index (complies with the Climate Bonds Taxonomy and the China Green Bond Endorsed Project Catalogue).

As of October 2015, according to CBI/HSBC (2015), 60% of total green bond issuance to date has officially incorporated a second-party review, and this percentage was stable over the three previous years. "Most" of the remaining 40% of green bonds use a type of proxy for second-party review, including audited assurance reports or benchmark measures related to use of proceeds and impact (e.g. LEED) (CBI/HSBC, 2015). For instance, the European Investment Bank (EIB), currently the largest green bond issuer, reports in detail on the allocations of its Climate Awareness Bond proceeds in annual audited sustainability reports and in a dedicated newsletter. According to the CBI, 96% of outstanding green bonds produce annual reports within one year of issuance, with 90% of the reports disclosing proceed allocation and climate impacts of projects or assets financed. According to Barclays (2015), there is greater investor demand for the bonds of issuers that provide high-quality information about the environmental benefits of the underwritten projects. However, according to Bloomberg (as reported at the June 2016 Green Bond Principles Conference) some 20% of issuers still self-label what constitutes a green bond, foregoing the use of an independent review. This has decreased from 40% in 2014 according to the CBI's figures. This highlights the need for continued attention on promoting transparency and environmental integrity, as discussed in Chapter 2.

Governments have also supported the development of standards and definitions for green bonds. In 2015, the Peoples' Bank of China (PBoC, China's central bank) released the first country-specific green bond issuance guidelines along with a taxonomy in the form of a "Green Bond Endorsed Project Catalogue" to guide financial sector issuance on green bonds in China (Box 1.6). In January 2016, India issued rules that will govern the issuance of green bonds locally. As part of the French Energy Transition Bill and National Low-Carbon Strategy (SNBC), an "energy transition for climate" label that is consistent with the GBPs will help identify investment funds that are funding the green economy (French Government, 2015). A methodology for project selection under the Dutch Green Funds Scheme also exists.

Box 1.6. Green bonds in China

The Peoples' Bank of China (PBoC) has estimated that green development in China will require annual investment of at least CNY 2 trillion (USD 305 billion) in the next years, with 85% of the financing needing to come from the private sector (PBoC/UNEP, 2015). In July 2015, the PBoC launched the Green Finance Committee (GFC), a multi-sectoral group tasked with investigating green finance reforms. The GFC, which is comprised of 85 members representing 65% of China's financial assets, has 6 main areas of research, with working parties addressing issues such as green banks, green bonds, responsible investment, etc.

In China, the green bond market is regulated by the PBoC, which issued regulations for the issuance and trading of green bonds in China's inter-bank bond market in December 2015. The regulations are broadly consistent with the Green Bond Principles (GBPs). The PBoC also published a Green Projects Catalogue, developed by the GFC and the China Society for Finance & Banking, which defines the assets and projects that qualify for green bond financing. The definitions cover the areas of energy conservation, pollution control, resources utilisation, clean transport, clean energy and adaptation.

A 2016 issues paper by the Climate Bonds Initiative (CBI), the International Institute for Sustainable Development and the UK Foreign and Commonwealth Office (CBI/IISD/UK Foreign & Commonwealth Office, 2016) details the categories of qualifying green projects included in the Chinese guidelines that differ from practices in the international green bond markets, in particular fossil fuel projects, public transport projects that use fossil fuels, and certain supply chain investments, and sets out a roadmap for the next steps of the green bond guidelines in the Chinese domestic green bond market with the aim of harmonising these guidelines with international practice.

In October 2015, the Agricultural Bank of China issued the first Chinese mainland green bond. The USD 1 billion bond, listed on the London Stock Exchange, was given an "A" rating by Fitch. Following the release of the green bond regulation and as of January 2016, the PBoC had approved RMB 100 billion (USD 15 billion) of green bond issuance by the China Industrial Bank and the Shanghai Pudong Development Bank. Also in November 2016, Bank of Communications issued RMB 30 billion (USD 4.4 billion) of green bonds.

The trajectory of green bond governance

Securities and markets serve to link investors to investments; in many ways a green bond can be seen as a process as well as a financing instrument. The development of standardised definitions and transparent procedures for assessing the greenness of bonds should help investors and businesses with aligned objectives find each other through the green label. As such, the green label has been described as a "discovery tool" (CBI/HSBC, 2016) with the potential to reduce friction by allowing investors to find environmentally sustainable securities while minimising transaction costs incurred through the due diligence and research normally required to find and compare unlabelled bonds in the broader market. Better securities and market design lowers the cost of linking investors to investments. While the green bond market is still evolving, efficient instruments and markets do this at the lowest cost, which in turn maximises the flow of capital. All of the work that goes into defining what is to count as a green bond can be understood as important "spadework" in helping buyers and sellers to find each other.

For instance, in 2015 the EIB established a direct reporting link between its green bonds and the projects they finance. This improved level of information flow was achieved through better design and the upgrading of its internal procedures and IT infrastructure following extensive due diligence. The linkage enables improved impact reporting and is also a strategic response to investor demand for funds that enable enhanced reporting on the carbon impact of their portfolios, in anticipation of regulatory requirements such as a French law (Article 173 of the Energy Transition Bill) that will oblige institutional investors to disclose this information (Hirtenstein, 2015).[15] The World Bank Group, some issuers of municipal green bonds (e.g. Massachusetts) and others also report details on a project-by-project basis.

In the broader bond markets, issuances are large and finance a wide range of different projects and activities often spanning an entire company, and decisions on which projects will be funded change over the course of a bond's lifetime. This is often not tracked in a transparent manner for a typical bond. The transparency requirements for green bonds effectively oblige bond issuers to develop new information tracking systems and procedures. This provides transparency benefits that are relatively new to the market and specific to green bond investments (Wong and Eeles, 2014).

Convergence towards commonly accepted definitions of activities that qualify for the green bond label and reporting procedures will be essential to maximise the effectiveness, efficiency and integrity of the market (see Table 1.4). Efforts aimed at harmonising and streamlining definitions can serve to reduce these barriers and bureaucratic burdens. Striking a balance will be critical to: 1) reduce the risk that a proliferation of standards and a lack of a commonality will result in fragmentation and issuance of green bonds that do not merit a green label, which will undermine confidence in the market and jeopardise market growth; and 2) reduce the risk that efforts to regulate or harmonise standards, or develop a consensus standard, will impose higher green transaction costs than are needed to deliver good environmental outcomes, and that jeopardise market growth. Where standards differ, transparency will be critical to ensure investors understand the types of projects they are funding.

The harmonisation of green bond market guidelines and standards is currently proceeding through a combination of public consultations along with industry and official sector initiatives. There is active dialogue between market participants both within and outside of industry initiatives, through bilateral contacts, working groups and their own consultations. This is illustrated by the annual consultation of GBP members and observers, and the one conducted by the CBI on its Standard v2.0 during 2015.

At the EU level, supporting green bond finance through convergence of green bond standards based on market-led initiatives is on the EU's policy agenda under the Capital Markets Union.[16] China and the United Kingdom have also agreed to work towards enhancing consistency of global green bond approaches. Governor Mark Carney of the Bank of England announced in September 2016 (Carney, 2016) that authorities are now working with the private sector to develop a green bond term sheet with standardised terms and conditions to significantly improve the ease and efficiency of green bond issuance and simplify investor access to green bond markets in multiple currencies, thereby moving them into the mainstream of finance.[17] In October 2016, the Japanese Ministry of the Environment established a discussion group with a view to producing a Japanese green bond guideline by March 2017. The guideline will refer to internationally recognised green bond principles while taking into account the situation of the Japanese market, in order to facilitate issuance of and investment in green bonds in Japan while preventing "green washing". Switzerland became the first national government member of the Climate Bond Partners to support the development of the Climate Bonds Standard (Kidney, 2015).

Green bonds were a feature of the Chinese G20 Presidency in 2016. The G20 "Green finance synthesis report" (G20, 2016a) which was welcomed in the Leaders' Statement at Hangzhou, outlined voluntary options to enhance the ability of the financial system to mobilise private capital for green investment developed by the Green Finance Study Group (GFSG). The Leaders' Statement (G20, 2016b) contains language referring to green bonds in paragraph 21: "We believe efforts could be made to... provide clear strategic policy signals and frameworks, promote voluntary principles for green finance, support the development of local green bond markets and promote international collaboration to facilitate cross-border investment in green bonds". The work of the GFSG was informed by a background paper produced by the OECD, the ICMA, the CBI and China GFC (OECD et al., 2016) that outlined suggested improvements on current practice regarding green bond guidelines and standards and can be referred to for a more comprehensive discussion of the issues touched on in this report.

The growing green bond market

Characteristics of green bonds

For the purposes of this analysis, green bonds are categorised into seven distinct forms that can be issued by different entities and as different structures or "types" (Box 1.7). The green bond market has materialised out of a variety of institutional actions. In 2007, the EIB launched a structured product "Climate Awareness Bond". Instead of a fixed coupon, the bond's returns were linked to an equity index (such a bond is commonly referred to in the bond market as "structured "). In 2008, the World Bank and Skandinaviska Enskilda Banken (SEB) launched the first labeled green bond together with a group of Swedish investors with mainstream financial mandates to participate in climate financing and raise awareness on climate related risk. The inaugural World Bank Green Bond was the first climate-related fixed income instrument to attract mainstream portfolios in a larger way (World Bank, n.d.).

The identical financial characteristics of green bonds compared to conventional bonds and the relatively simple principle of green labelling and the ring-fencing, earmarking or "use of proceeds" implied by the label have been catalytic elements in the market's growth. Combined, they have allowed for a wide range of issuers and investors to join the market attracted by the advantages offered by green bonds (see Table 1.4).

Box 1.7. **The seven types of green bonds**

1. **Corporate bond:** A "use of proceeds" bond issued by a corporate entity with recourse to the issuer in the case of default on interest payments or on return of principal. This category includes bonds issued by "YieldCo" vehicles to finance asset acquisitions.
2. **Project bond:** A bond backed by single or multiple projects for which the investor has direct exposure to the risk of the project, with or without recourse to the bond issuer.
3. **Asset-backed security (ABS):** A bond collateralised by one or more specific projects, usually providing recourse only to the assets, except in the case of covered bonds (included in this category). For covered bonds, the primary recourse is to the issuing entity, with secondary recourse to an underlying cover pool of assets, in the event of default of the issuer.
4. **Supranational, sub-sovereign and agency (SSA) bond:** Bonds issued by international financial institutions (IFIs) such as the World Bank and the European Investment Bank (i.e. "supranational issuers"). SSA bonds have features similar to a corporate bond relating to "use of proceeds" and recourse to the issuer. Agency bonds are included in this category (e.g. issuance by export-import banks), as are sub-sovereign national development banks (e.g. the German KfW).
5. **Municipal bond:** Bonds issued by a municipal government, region or city.
6. **Sovereign bond:** Bonds issued by a national government. In December 2016, Poland issued the first sovereign green bond, followed by the launch of a sovereign green bond by France in January 2017. A number of other countries also have indicated their intention to issue sovereign green bonds.
7. **Financial sector bond:** A type of corporate bond issued by a financial institution to raise capital specifically to finance "on-balance sheet lending" (i.e. to provide loans) to green activities (e.g. ABN AMRO or Agricultural Bank of China). This type of bond is considered separately for the purposes of OECD scenario modelling to retain a distinction between financial sector bond issuances which finance lending and those which directly finance green investments.

Green bond market evolution

The market evolved beyond SSA issuers in 2013, when corporate issuers joined the market, with Vasakronan (a Swedish real estate company), then Bank of America's "financial sector" bond, followed by Électricité de France (EDF) and others. Corporates have also extended the green bond label to asset-backed securities (ABS), with Toyota's 2014 sale of securities with proceeds used for investment in electric vehicles and hybrids. The deal was backed by leases and loans to non-green vehicles, as the pool of leases and loans to electric vehicles and hybrids was too small.

Municipalities have joined the market, with the issuance by Île-de-France (the Paris region) in 2012 followed by Gothenburg (Sweden) in 2013. The year 2014 also saw the first emerging market municipal issuance, by Johannesburg (South Africa). Export credit agencies and export-import banks have issued green bonds including in India (India ExIM). The first ABS were issued by Hannon Armstrong (a US real estate investment trust providing debt and equity financing to the energy efficiency and renewable energy markets) in 2013 backed by 100 individual wind, solar and energy efficiency infrastructure installations at 20 properties, and the covered bond issuance (Berlin HYP) occurred in 2015 along with further growth in ABS and project bonds. In 2015, corporate bonds moved beyond the utilities and real estate sectors to include transport and waste, with a GBP 400 million green bond from Transport for London and a EUR 480 million issuance from French recycling company Paprec. In 2016, the first technology company issued a labelled green bond, with Apple's USD 1.5 billion green bond backing renewable energy for data centres, energy efficiency and green materials. The seven-year security, with a coupon of 2.85%, is the first green bond from the world's largest consumer electronics company and the largest single issue from a corporation unconnected to electricity generation. In December 2016, Poland became the first country to issue a sovereign green bond of EUR 750 million to fund renewable energy, clean transportation, sustainable agriculture, afforestation, national parks and reclamation of heaps (State Treasury of Poland, 2016). In January 2017, France also launched its sovereign green bond following prior announcements in 2016. EUR 10 billion of expenditure has been identified as eligible for green bond allocation based on the "energy transition for climate" label issued by the French government (French Ministry of Economy and Finance, 2017). The first issuance amounted to EUR 7 billion.

Box 1.8. Green bonds currently have financial features that are identical to conventional bonds

With the exception of the ring-fencing or earmarking of proceeds required by the green label, green bonds have financial characteristics that are identical to conventional bonds from the same issuer, including the credit quality, yield and price at which they are issued.

The concept of "flat-pricing" has been central to the rapid, demand-driven expansion of the market. Prices are said to be "flat" at issuance (relative to most regular, simple and standardised ["plain vanilla"] bonds from the same issuer) because the credit profile of a green bond is the same as any "plain vanilla" bonds from the same issuer, so no difference in pricing is warranted. This means that issuers have not been able or willing to realise pricing advantages (and a correspondingly lower cost of capital for green projects) through green labelling as investors are unwilling to take lower than expected returns at the primary issuance stage simply for the ability to "go green" (BNEF, 2014). At the same time, investors have not been able to realise demand for higher yields to justify supposed additional risk-taking to finance green activities, as in general (with exception for project, covered and asset-backed securities [ABS] bonds) they are financing the balance sheet of the issuing entity itself (so the credit risk is the same as any other regular bond from the same entity).

Yet, one report has indicated that green bonds trade on the secondary market at a slight premium during certain periods studied (Barclays, 2015). Barclays partly attributes this phenomenon to "opportunistic pricing based on strong demand from environmentally focused funds faced with comparatively limited green bond supply" along with other factors that are difficult to substantiate empirically at present (Barclays, 2015). The World Bank (2015: 44) reports that "anecdotally, investors in green bonds have been able to sell at higher prices than conventional bonds because of the rarity of green bonds". CBI/HSBC (2016) report that anecdotal evidence has emerged that, in some markets at least, green bonds are receiving better pricing than plain vanilla bonds.

A mix of views exists on how market pricing for green bonds will develop. Issuers see strong demand to the point of oversubscription and argue for a pricing advantage relative to vanilla bonds to compensate for green bond-specific issuance costs, while investors are unwilling to accept a materially lower yield (or a higher price) that cannot be sufficiently justified on a risk-adjusted return basis. The green bond market is evolving under pressure from issuers looking to drive the costs of issuance down and investors calling for more supply to meet their demand. CBI/HSBC (2016) takes the view that pricing will (and should) remain tight, but within limits acceptable to the majority of investors. Beyond this, they argue, green investments should and will be preferenced using government policy tools.

Much attention has been focused on the pricing of green corporate bonds, but as discussed in this report, there are many different types of green bonds (see Box 1.7). Different levels of recourse exist, and bonds will price accordingly. For instance, corporate "use of proceeds" bonds differently to project bonds and ABS.

Green bond issuing entities can make use of a variety of structures related to the "use of proceeds" (according to the GBP, four "types" of green bond at present, although additional types may emerge). The most common structures used have been standard "recourse-to-the-issuer" debt obligations (i.e. if the principal is not returned to the investor in full for whatever reason, the investor can recoup unreturned principal from the issuer). While the use of funds is targeted, the repayment obligation is backed by all of the issuer's assets. Most SSA and corporate green bonds are characterised by this "plain vanilla" structure. Green bonds can also be backed by specific cash flows which are pledged as the basis for repayment (such as the revenue of a project); may be issued by a special purpose entity responsible for a specific project and without recourse to the issuer; or can be a securitisation with collateral from a collection of many assets.

Within the unlabelled market, there is a small but growing pocket of bonds whose cash flows depend on the underlying projects, unlike corporate and SSA bonds where cash flows depend on the issuer and may not necessarily be linked to projects. These unlabelled green project bonds and ABS totalled about USD 15 billion in 2014 according to CBI/HSBC (2015). In practice less than USD 2 billion of the USD 15 billion in ABS included as climate-aligned bonds have been self-labelled as green[18] and few project or covered bonds have been labelled as such.

The geography of the green bond market is expanding and diversifying (Box 1.9). As of February 2016, green bonds had been issued in 25 jurisdictions, including 22 for domestic and foreign investors, and 3 for foreign investors only. Green bonds have been issued in 23 currencies and in 14 markets of the G20. Annex 1.A1 includes further details on country experiences with green bonds.

Box 1.9. The geography of the green bond market

Green bonds issued for domestic and foreign investors: Australia; Austria; Canada; the People's Republic of China; Denmark; Estonia; France; Germany; Hong Kong, China; India; Italy; Japan; Latvia; Mexico; the Netherlands; Norway; Peru; South Africa; Spain; Sweden; the United Kingdom; and the United States.

For foreign investors only: Brazil, Switzerland and Chinese Taipei.

G20 markets: Australia, Brazil, Canada, China, the European Union, France, Germany, India, Italy, Japan, Mexico, South Africa, the United Kingdom and the United States.

Currencies: AUD, BRL, CAD, CHF, COP, EUR, GBP, HUF, IDR, INR, JPY, MXN, MYR, NOK, NZD, PEN, PLN, RMB, RUB, SEK, TRY, USD, ZAR.

The benefits of green bonds

Green bonds offer advantages and disadvantages in their use and these are compiled in Table 1.4. At a more general level, the green bond market can offer several important benefits for green investment by the public and private sectors as outlined in OECD et al. (2016). These include:

1. **Providing an additional source of green financing.** Given immense green investment needs, bonds are one appropriate financing instrument to address such projects. As traditional sources of debt financing will not be sufficient in light of immense green investment needs, there is a need to introduce new means of financing that can leverage a wider investor base including institutional investors (such as pension funds, insurance companies and sovereign wealth funds) that

manage over USD 100 trillion in assets globally. The development of the green bond market can provide an additional source of funding to green lending by banks and green equity financing by investors.

2. **Enabling more long-term green financing by addressing maturity mismatch.** In many countries, the ability of banks to provide long-term green loans is constrained due to the short maturity of their liabilities and a lack of instruments for hedging duration risks. Corporates that can only access short-term bank credit also face refinancing risks for long-term green projects. If banks and corporates can issue medium- and long-term green bonds for green projects, these constraints on long-term green financing can be mitigated.

3. **Enhancing issuers' reputation and clarifying environmental strategy.** Issuing a green bond is an effective way to develop and implement a credible sustainability strategy for investors and the general public by clarifying how proceeds raised will contribute to a pipeline of tangible environmental projects. Green bonds can thus help enhance an issuer's reputation along with internal sustainable development policies, as this is an effective way for the issuer to display its commitment towards improving environmental sustainability. These enhancements may result in benefits for product marketing as well as potential government policy incentives for business operations. Setting up a green bond framework also can serve to upgrade issuers' environmental risk management process due to their commitment to "green" disclosure.

4. **Offering potential cost advantages.** While the cost advantage is not yet evident in the current nascent green bond market, it is possible that, once the market attracts a wider investor base both domestically and internationally, a differentiated pricing for green bonds vs. regular bonds may emerge provided demand is sustained. According to the CBI, a number of issuers also report a benefit in the increased speed of "book building" (i.e. the process of generating, capturing and recording investor demand for a bond issue), which translates into reduced costs for marketing and road shows. In some countries, government incentives such as tax reduction, interest subsidies and credit guarantees are also being discussed as options for further reducing the funding costs for green bonds, with the United States having already experimented in this area with green property bonds and municipal bonds.

5. **Facilitating the "greening" of traditionally brown sectors.** The aforementioned benefits of the green bond market can function as a transition mechanism that encourages issuers in less environmentally friendly sectors to take part in the green bond market (provided they ring-fence proceeds for green projects) and also to reduce their environmental footprint by engaging in green investment activities that can be funded via a green bond. This complements mandatory "real economy" policies that lead to changes in business models (such as carbon pricing, waste reduction and recycling targets, policies to promote the circular economy, etc.)

6. **Making new green financial products available to responsible and long-term investors.** Pension funds, insurance companies, sovereign wealth funds and other institutional investors that have a special preference for sustainable (responsible) investment and long-term investment are looking for new financial instruments to achieve their investment targets. The green label is a discovery mechanism that lowers the "search costs" for investors looking for green opportunities in a vast ocean of bonds. Green bonds provide these investors with the access to such

products and a way for many other investors to diversify their portfolios. At the same time, numerous green bond issuers report an improved diversification of their investor base, thereby expanding their funding sources and potentially reducing exposure to "funding risk" and bond demand fluctuations.

Table 1.4. **Advantages and disadvantages of green bonds as cited by investors and issuers**

For investors	
Advantages	Disadvantages
Commonly cited	
– Investors can balance risk-adjusted financial returns with environmental benefits – Satisfies environment, social and governance (ESG) requirements and green investment mandates – Improved risk assessment in an otherwise opaque fixed income market through use of proceeds reporting – Potential use of pure-play, project and asset-backed securities as instruments to actively hedge against climate policy risks in a portfolio that includes emissions-intensive assets (see Annex 1.A2) – Recognised by the UNFCCC as non-state actor "climate action"	– Small and nascent (and potentially less liquid) market, small bond sizes – Lack of unified standards can create confusion and possibility for reputational risk if green integrity of bond questioned – Limited scope for legal enforcement of green integrity – Lack of standardisation can lead to complexities in research and a need for extra due diligence that may not always be fulfilled
Infrequently cited	
– Engagement and private dialogue with issuers on ESG topics related to green bond issuance results in information that enhances credit analysis, through more comprehensive credit profiles of borrowers – Added transparency of use of proceeds and reporting requirements provides informational advantage otherwise unavailable (on spending efficiency, project details and updates, impact performance) which gives green bond investors a significant information advantage (Wong and Eeles, 2014) – Tracking of use of proceeds and reporting leads to improved internal governance structures and a positive feedback loop which improves the overall credit quality of the issuer (Wong and Eeles, 2014)	
For issuers	
Advantages	Disadvantages
Commonly cited	
– Demonstrating and implementing issuer's approach to ESG issues – Improving diversification of a bond issuer's investor base, thereby expanding funding sources and potentially reducing exposure to bond demand fluctuations – Strong investor demand can lead to oversubscription and potential to increase issuance size – Evidence of greater proportion of "buy and hold" investors for green bonds which can lead to lower bond volatility in secondary market – Reputational benefits (e.g. marketing can highlight issuer's green credentials and support for green investment) – Articulation and enhanced credibility of sustainability strategy (putting one's "money where their mouth is") leading to enhanced dialogue with investors – Access to "economies of scale" as majority of issuance costs are in setting up the processes	– Upfront and ongoing transaction costs from labelling and associated administrative, certification, reporting, verification and monitoring requirements (cost estimates vary) – Reputational risk if a bond's green credentials are challenged
Infrequently cited	
– Tracking of use of proceeds and reporting leads to improved internal governance structures, communication and knowledge sharing between project side and treasury side of business (Wong and Eeles, 2014) – For municipalities, a tool to reach constituencies physically located close to the green project they intend to support and provide them with opportunities to invest in programmes that have direct proximal impact (World Bank, 2015)	– Investors may seek penalties for a "green default" whereby a bond is paid in full but issuer breaks agreed green clauses (KPMG, 2015)

Notes

1. For the purposes of this report, the term green infrastructure includes: 1) "low-carbon and climate-resilient" infrastructure projects, which either mitigate greenhouse gas emissions or support adaptation to climate change or both; 2) "sustainable energy infrastructure", which as defined in OECD (2015) includes the following sectors: power generation from solar, wind, small hydro, geothermal, marine, biomass and waste-to-energy, biofuels, carbon capture and sequestration and energy smart technologies (such as smart grids, interconnectors, energy efficiency, storage and electric vehicles); and 3) other investments, including sustainable agriculture, floodplain levees and coastal protection, waste management infrastructure and "green" water infrastructure (OECD, 2016). Green water infrastructure may include wastewater treatment and infrastructure that requires less concrete, e.g. through rainwater harvesting, source control of surface water (such as sustainable urban drainage systems), green roofs, and local processing of grey or black water.

2. Estimates of additional investment requirements typically do not consider returns on investment through lower operating costs due to energy savings from efficiency investments or lower fuel costs in the case of renewable energy replacing fossil energy. They also do not consider other benefits such as lower health costs. One study (Kennedy and Corfee-Morlot, 2012) estimates that shifting to low-carbon and climate-resilient infrastructure could result in systemic change that raises only slightly, or even lowers, overall investment costs. Investing in sustainable energy also makes economic sense. The IEA (2014) presents evidence that the USD 44 trillion in additional investment needed to decarbonise the energy system in line with the "2 degree scenario" by 2050 is more than offset by over USD 115 trillion in fuel savings – resulting in net savings of USD 71 trillion.

3. As context, the global project finance market for all types of infrastructure included USD 298 billion in loans and USD 55 billion in bonds in 2013 (S&P, 2014).

4. As described in Box 1.2, a bond raises upfront capital from investors in return for periodic "fixed income" in the form of interest rate "coupon" payments. There are other forms of coupon structure including, "zero" coupon, fixed rate, floating rate, index linked, coupon linked to environmental performance and others. Investors are also eventually returned their initial investment (the "principal") when the bond reaches its maturity. The periodic coupon payments can match well with the cash flows generated by infrastructure assets.

5. The spread varies across regions and changes due to economic and market conditions. For instance, as of November 2015 in the United Kingdom (broadly representative of EU and OECD markets as London is the most active project finance lending market globally) the all-in cost of a 20-year project loan compared with a project bond of a similar credit quality (e.g. BBB-) may be roughly as follows: Loan: Libor (~250 basis points (bps)) + ~250 bps credit spread (~5%). Bond: "mid-swaps" (~150 bps) + ~300bp credit spread (~4.5%). Therefore project loans are more expensive than equivalent project bonds reflecting low yields in the mid-swap market (the benchmark for bond pricing). At the same time, demand for investment-grade project debt in the bank market has been high so credit spreads have been declining, making pricing very competitive with the bond market, but only up to 20 years of loan tenor. Typically banks are not prepared to go beyond 20 years, which is where the bond market is more competitive for project financing and refinancing (Source: S&P, interviews).

6. OECD Global Pension Statistics, Global Insurance Statistics and Institutional Investors databases, and OECD estimates.

7. SEB analysis provided to OECD based on Bloomberg data.

8. i.e. those bonds that have been issued and have not reached maturity or been redeemed.

9. For instance, traditional bonds of "pure-play" wind and solar energy companies qualify as unlabelled green bonds. Some issuers may choose not to label bonds as green due to concerns over a lack of standardisation in the market, political or stakeholder sensitivities and concerns over restrictions associated with the label.

10. In addition to the USD 42 billion of green bonds issued throughout the course of 2015, the BNEF identified an extra USD 6 billion of such bonds (wind and solar project bonds and asset-backed securities) and designated them as green bonds via a tag on the Bloomberg Terminal.

11. The GBP recommend that the term "green bonds" be used only for GBP-aligned bonds while the wider universe should be referred to as climate or environmental themed bonds. For the statistics cited in this report the green bond definition used is cited as well.

12. According to the GBP, these broad categories include, but are not limited to: renewable energy (including production, transmission, appliances and products); energy efficiency (such as in new and refurbished buildings, energy storage, district heating, smart grids, appliances and products); pollution prevention and control (including wastewater treatment, greenhouse gas control, soil remediation, recycling and waste-to-energy, value-added products from waste and remanufacturing, and associated environmental monitoring analysis); sustainable management of living natural resources (including sustainable agriculture, fishery, aquaculture, forestry and climate smart farm inputs such as biological crop protection or drip irrigation); terrestrial and aquatic biodiversity conservation (including the protection of coastal, marine and watershed environments); clean transportation (such as electric, hybrid, public, rail, non-motorised, multi-modal transportation, infrastructure for clean energy vehicles and reduction of harmful emissions); sustainable water management (including sustainable infrastructure for clean and/or drinking water, sustainable urban drainage systems and river training and other forms of flooding mitigation); climate change adaptation (including information support systems, such as climate observation and early warning systems); eco-efficient products, production technologies and processes (such as development and introduction of environmentally friendlier, eco-labelled or certified products, resource-efficient packaging and distribution).

14. According to the World Bank (2015), the market has been relying on a variety of issuer disclosures, second opinions and commentary from academics, investment advisers, auditors, technical experts, index providers (see Box 1.4), the media and non-governmental organisations including organisations such as CICERO, the Climate Bonds Initiative, the DNB, Oekom, Sustainalytics, and Vigeo, among others.

15. See: www.eib.org/investor_relations/cab/index.htm.

16. A recent study by the European Commission recommends supporting a common European Green Bonds Standard building on existing market-led initiatives (European Commission, 2016).

17. Specific issues under discussion include: 1) ensuring use of proceeds is clearly delineated for a green project or activity; 2) issuers having a clearly defined process to validate proceeds are being used for intended and stated purpose; 3) a clear, transparent and regular mechanism for reporting the use of proceeds, often involving second- or third-party verification; and 4) an appropriate dispute mechanism for when these other conditions are not met.

18. e.g. Toyota, Fannie Mae, Hannon Armstrong & Renew Financial.

References

Alvarez, A. et al. (2013), "Between deluge and drought: Liquidity and funding for Asian banks", *McKinsey Working Papers on Risk*, No. 45, McKinsey & Company, www.mckinsey.com/~/media/mckinsey%20offices/india/pdfs/between_deluge_and_drought.ashx.

Banktrack (2015), "Open letter on the 2015 update of the Green Bond Principles", 30 April, www.banktrack.org/download/150430_open_letter_to_green_bond_principles_pdf/150430_open_letter_to_green_bond_principles.pdf.

Barclays (2015), "The cost of being green", *US Credit Focus*, 18 September, www.environmental-finance.com/assets/files/US_Credit_Focus_The_Cost_of_Being_Green.pdf.

Bielenberg, A. et al. (2016), "Financing change: How to mobilize private sector financing for sustainable infrastructure", McKinsey & Company Center for Business and Environment, January, http://newclimateeconomy.report/2015/wp-content/uploads/sites/3/2016/01/Financing_change_How_to_mobilize_private-sector_financing_for_sustainable-_infrastructure.pdf.

BNEF (2014), "Green bonds market outlook 2014: Blooming with new varietals", Bloomberg New Energy Finance, 2 June, http://about.bnef.com/white-papers/green-bonds-market-outlook-2014/content/uploads/sites/4/2014/06/2014-06-02-Green-bonds-market-outlook-2014.pdf.

Boissinot, J., D. Huber and G. Lame (2016), "Finance and climate: The transition to a low-carbon and climate-resilient economy from a financial sector perspective", *OECD Journal: Financial Market Trends*, Vol. 2015/1, OECD Publishing, Paris, http://dx.doi.org/10.1787/fmt-2015-5jrrz76d5td5.

Buehler, K., P. Noteboom and D. Williams (2013), "Between deluge and drought: The future of US bank liquidity and funding", *McKinsey Working Papers on Risk*, No. 48, McKinsey & Company, www.mckinsey.com/~/media/mckinsey/dotcom/client_service/Risk/Working%20papers/48_Future%20of%20US%20funding.ashx.

Caldecott, B. (2012), "Green infrastructure bonds: Accessing the scale of low cost capital required to tackle climate change", Climate Change Capital.

Carney, M. (2016), "Resolving the climate paradox", Speech given by Mark Carney, Governor of the Bank of England and Chair of the Financial Stability Board, 22 September, www.fsb.org/wp-content/uploads/Resolving-the-climate-paradox.pdf.

CBI (2016), "Final year end green bond market roundup report", www.climatebonds.net/files/files/2015%20GB%20Market%20Roundup%2003A.pdf.

CBI/HSBC (2016), "Bonds and climate change: The state of the market in 2016", Climate Bonds Initiative and HSBC, July, www.climatebonds.net/files/files/CBI%20State%20of%20the%20Market%202016%20A4.pdf.

CBI/HSBC (2015), "Bonds and climate change: The state of the market in 2015", Climate Bonds Initiative and HSBC, July, www.climatebonds.net/files/files/CBI-HSBC%20report%207July%20JG01.pdf.

CBI/IISD/UK Foreign & Commonwealth Office (2016), "Roadmap for China: Green bond guidelines for the next stage of market growth", Climate Bonds Initiative and International Institute for Sustainable Development, https://www.climatebonds.net/files/files/CBI-IISD-Paper1-Final-01C_A4.pdf.

Ceres (2015), "A statement of investor expectations for the green bond market", Statement from the Investor Network on Climate Risk, www.ceres.org/files/investor-files/statement-of-investor-expectations-for-green-bonds/at_download/file.

Clapp, C. and A. Torvanger (2015), "CICERO grades climate-friendly bonds with shades of green, April", news post, CICERO, 30 March.

Deutsche Bank (2015), Dinner speech of Caio Koch-Weser at the Workshop of the G7 countries at the level of department heads, 22 April.

Dobbs, R. et al. (2013), "Infrastructure productivity: How to save $1 trillion a year", McKinsey & Company, January, www.mckinsey.com/~/media/McKinsey/dotcom/Insights%20and%20pubs/MGI/Research/Urbanization/Infrastructure%20productivity/MGI_Infrastructure_Full_report_Jan2013.ashx.

European Commission (2016), *Study on the Potential of Green Bond Finance for Resource-Efficient Investments*, Publications Office of the European Union, Luxembourg, http://ec.europa.eu/environment/enveco/pdf/potential-green-bond.pdf.

ECB (2015), "Consolidated banking data", Database, *ECB Statistical Data Warehouse*.

French Government (2015), "Adoption of the national low-carbon strategy for climate", 27 November, www.gouvernement.fr/en/adoption-of-the-national-low-carbon-strategy-for-climate.

French Ministry of Economy and Finance (2017), "Structuration de la première obligation verte souveraine" ["Structure of the first sovereign green bond"], Ministry of Economy and Finance, 3 January, http://proxy-pubminefi.diffusion.finances.gouv.fr/pub/document/18/21952.pdf.

G20 (2016a), "G20 green finance synthesis report", G20 Green Finance Study Group, 5 September, http://unepinquiry.org/wp-content/uploads/2016/09/Synthesis_Report_Full_EN.pdf.

G20 (2016b), "G20 Leaders' Communiqué", Hangzhou Summit, 4-5 September, http://unepinquiry.org/wp-content/uploads/2017/01/2016-09-04-g20-communique-en.pdf.

Gerken, A. et al. (2013), "Between deluge and drought: The divided future of European bank-funding markets", *McKinsey Working Papers on Risk*, No. 41, McKinsey & Company, March, www.mckinsey.com/~/media/McKinsey/dotcom/client_service/Risk/Working%20papers/41_Between_deluge_and_drought.ashx.

Gilbert, K. (2015), "Underwriters pull back slowing rise of green bond market", Institutional Investor, 25 September, www.institutionalinvestor.com/article/3491673/asset-management-fixed-income/underwriters-pull-back-slowing-rise-of-green-bond-market.html#.WIih9BvhCUk.

Global Sustainable Investment Alliance (2015), "Global sustainable investment review 2014", 24 February, Bloomberg, www.gsi-alliance.org/wp-content/uploads/2015/02/GSIA_Review_download.pdf.

Green City Bonds Coalition (2015), "How to issue a green muni bond: The green muni bonds playbook", www.climatebonds.net/files/files/Green%20City%20Playbook.pdf.

Hirtenstein, A. (2015), "EIB links green bonds to projects in push for climate", Bloomberg, 5 October, www.bloomberg.com/news/articles/2015-10-05/eib-links-green-bonds-to-projects-in-second-push-for-climate.

ICMA (2016), "Green Bond Principles, 2016: Voluntary process guidelines for issuing green bonds", International Capital Market Association, 16 June, www.icmagroup.org/Regulatory-Policy-and-Market-Practice/green-bonds/green-bond-principles.

ICMA (2015), "Green bonds: Working towards a harmonized framework for impact reporting", International Capital Market Association, December, www.icmagroup.org/assets/documents/Regulatory/Green-Bonds/20151202-0530-FINALRevised-Proposal.pdf.

IEA (2016), *Medium-Term Renewable Energy Market Report 2016*, International Energy Agency, Paris, http://dx.doi.org/10.1787/renewmar-2016-en.

IEA (2015), *World Energy Outlook 2015*, OECD Publishing, Paris, http://dx.doi.org/10.1787/weo-2015-en.

IEA (2014), *World Energy Investment Outlook*, OECD/IEA, Paris, www.iea.org/publications/freepublications/publication/WEIO2014.pdf.

Inderst, G. et al. (2012), "Defining and measuring green investments: Implications for institutional investors' asset allocations", *OECD Working Papers on Finance, Insurance and Private Pensions*, No. 24, OECD Publishing, Paris, http://dx.doi.org/10.1787/5k9312twnn44-en.

Kaminker, C. and F. Stewart (2012), "The role of institutional investors in financing clean energy", *OECD Working Papers on Finance, Insurance and Private Pensions*, No. 23, OECD Publishing, Paris, http://dx.doi.org/10.1787/5k9312v2116f-en.

Kennedy, C. and J. Corfee-Morlot (2012), "Mobilising investment in low carbon, climate resilient infrastructure", *OECD Environment Working Papers*, No. 46, OECD Publishing, Paris, http://dx.doi.org/10.1787/5k8zm3gxxmnq-en.

Kidney, S. (2015), "Switzerland joins as Climate Bonds Partner + announces grant funding for climate bond standards development. Wow! Danke! Merci! Grazie! Grazia!", Blog, 15 July, https://www.climatebonds.net/2015/07/switzerland-joins-climate-bonds-partner-announces-grant-funding-climate-bond-standards#sthash.zH1L4jFP.dpuf.

KPMG (2015), "Gearing up for green bonds: Key considerations for bond issuers", https://assets.kpmg.com/content/dam/kpmg/pdf/2015/03/gearing-up-for-green-bonds-v1.pdf.

NCE (2015), *Seizing the Global Opportunity: Partnerships for Better Growth and Better Climate*, Global Commission on the Economy and Climate, New Climate Economy, Washington, DC and London, http://newclimateeconomy.report/2015/wp-content/uploads/2014/08/NCE-2015_Seizing-the-Global-Opportunity_web.pdf.

OECD (2016), "Progress report on approaches to mobilising institutional investment for green infrastructure", OECD, Paris, http://unepinquiry.org/wp-content/uploads/2016/09/11_Progress_Report_on_Approaches_to_Mobilising_Institutional_Investment_for_Green_Infrastructure.pdf.

OECD (2015), *Mapping Channels to Mobilise Institutional Investment in Sustainable Energy*, Green Finance and Investment, OECD Publishing, Paris, http://dx.doi.org/10.1787/9789264224582-en.

OECD (2013), "Long-term investors and green infrastructure", *Policy Highlights* brochure, OECD, Paris, www.oecd.org/env/cc/Investors%20in%20Green%20Infrastructure%20brochure%20(f)%20[lr].pdf.

OECD et al. (2016) "Green bonds: Country experiences, barriers and options", OECD/ICMA/CBI/China GFC, http://unepinquiry.org/wp-content/uploads/2016/09/6_Green_Bonds_Country_Experiences_Barriers_and_Options.pdf.

PBoC/UNEP (2015), "Establishing China's green financial system", Final Report to the Green Finance Task Force, The People's Bank of China and United Nations Environment Programme, April, www.cbd.int/financial/privatesector/china-Green%20Task%20Force%20Report.pdf.

Pooler, M. (2014), "EU banks back in infrastructure loan zone", *Financial Times*, 24 May, www.ft.com/cms/s/0/2d625268-e0ef-11e3-a934-00144feabdc0.html.

Roxburgh, C., S. Lund and J. Piotrowski (2011), *Mapping Global Capital Markets 2011*, McKinsey & Company, August, www.mckinsey.com/industries/private-equity-and-principal-investors/our-insights/mapping-global-capital-markets-2011.

S&P (Standard & Poor's Ratings Services) (2014), "Global infrastructure: How to fill a $500 billion hole", Standard & Poor's Financial Services LLC, 16 January, www.engagedinvestor.co.uk/Journals/2014/01/30/n/a/q/How-To-Fill-A.pdf.

State Treasury of Poland (2016), "Green bond framework", 5 December, www.finanse.mf.gov.pl/documents/766655/c7ef4509-80ee-41e6-8dca-084250f63b6b.

UNFCCC (2015), "Report of the Conference of the Parties on its twentieth session, held in Lima 1 to 14 December 2014: Addendum: Part two: Action taken by the Conference of the Parties at its twentieth session", FCCC/CP/2014/10/Add. 1, United Nations Framework Convention on Climate Change, http://unfccc.int/documentation/documents/advanced_search/items/6911.php?priref=600008358.

WEF (2013), "Reducing the cost of capital for green projects", webpage, http://reports.weforum.org/green-investing-2013/reducing-the-cost-of-capital-for-green-projects/?doing_wp_cron=1455210036.523138999389648437500.

Wilkie, T. (2015), "Green bonds and growing pains", *Global Capital*, 29 September, www.globalcapital.com/article/tjkj89ztn6kf/green-bonds-and-growing-pains.

Wong, L. and J. Eeles (2014), "Green bonds go mainstream", Nikko Asset Management, 4 December, https://emea.nikkoam.com/articles/2014/12/green-bonds-go-mainstream.

World Bank (n.d.), "Why did multilateral development banks (MDBs) issue the first green bonds?", webpage, The World Bank, http://treasury.worldbank.org/cmd/htm/Chapter-2-MDBs-and-Green-Bonds.html.

World Bank (2015), "What are green bonds?", The World Bank, Washington, DC, http://treasury.worldbank.org/cmd/htm/What-are-Green-Bonds-Home.html.

WWF (2016), "Les obligations vertes doivent tenir leurs promesses!" ["Green bonds must keep the green promise!"], WWF, Paris, http://awsassets.wwfffr.panda.org/downloads/20160610_synthese_green_bonds.pdf.

Zindler, E. and K. Locklin (2016), "Mapping the gap: The road from Paris", Bloomberg New Energy Finance, 27 January, http://docs.google.com/viewer?url=www.ceres.org/resources/reports/mapping-the-gap-the-road-from-paris/at_download/file&embedded=true.

Annex 1.A1.
Selected regional experiences with green bonds

Institutional investment in green bonds: The case of South Africa's Government Employees Pension Fund

The Government Employees Pension Fund (GEPF) is Africa's largest pension fund, with over ZAR 1.5 trillion (USD 109 billion) in assets under management. The GEPF is also the largest investor in Johannesburg Stock Exchange-listed companies, owning on average 10% of companies listed on the Johannesburg Securities Exchange and around half of the government inflation-linked bonds outstanding.

The GEPF, a signatory to the UN-supported Principles for Responsible Investment states in its investment policy that 5% of its portfolio shall be set aside for developmental investments in the areas of economic infrastructure, social infrastructure, green economy projects, and small enterprise or black empowerment initiatives (GEPF, 2015). Over the years, the GEPF has invested in climate-aligned bonds in the following ways:

- In 2012, South Africa's state-owned Industrial Development Corporation issued a ZAR 5.2 billion green bond to finance clean energy projects. ZAR 1 billion of the bond was bought by the GEPF (GEPF, 2012).
- In 2013, Soitec issued a rand-denominated project bond to finance the Touwsrivier solar power plant using concentrated photovoltaic technology (Soitec, 2013). The unlabelled climate-aligned bond utilised an innovative amortizing repayment structure with a coupon rate of 11% over 15 years. The GEPF bought a 40% equity stake in the project.

United States: Municipal bonds

The American Society of Civil Engineers (2014) estimates that the United States will need to invest USD 3.6 trillion in infrastructure by 2020. Green bonds and other similar financial instruments present an opportunity for US public and private sectors to align their investments with sustainable objectives, without compromising their fiduciary responsibilities.

In Q1 2014, the United States' outstanding climate-themed bonds were estimated at USD 35.8 billion. Included in that universe were clean renewable energy bonds, which are tax credit bonds, created as part of 2005 Energy Tax Incentives Act (NREL, 2009). Clean renewable energy bonds are used to finance renewable energy projects, primarily in the public sector, and are nationally allocated and capped in volume. The bondholder receives federal tax credits in lieu of a portion of the traditional bond interest, resulting in a lower effective interest rate for the borrower.

Green municipal bonds in particular have gained traction in the United States since 2013, with activity from a wide array of stakeholders. In the United States, the green muni bond market grew from a single USD 100 million green muni bond issuance in 2013 to USD 2.5 billion of green muni bonds issued in 2014. As of October 2015, green muni bonds have been issued in the United States at the state, county and city levels. To provide clarity and guidance to prospective municipal issuers, the US branch of the Green City Bonds Coalition published the "Green muni bonds playbook" in July 2015. It contains a five-step guide for issuing a green muni bond, as well as an in-depth analysis of two case studies.

Table 1.A1.1. **Labelled green municipal bonds in the United States as of October 2015**

State bonds	County/regional bonds	City bonds
– Utah – Connecticut – Massachusetts (through Massachusetts State Clean Water, Massachusetts Development Authority and Commonwealth of Massachusetts) – District of Columbia Water – New York State Environmental Facilities – Indiana Finance Authority – Iowa Finance Authority – Hawaii – California	– Jefferson County, Colorado – East Bay Municipal Utility District, California – Hartford County, Connecticut – East Central Wastewater, Florida – Central Puget Sound Transit Authority	– City of Saint Paul, Minnesota – City of Los Angeles, California – City of Asheville, North Carolina – City of Venice, Florida – City of Chicago, Illinois (through Chicago Met Water and Chicago Board of Education) – City of Tacoma, Washington – Martha's Vineyard Land Bank – City of Spokane, Washington – City of San Francisco, California

Source: Climate Bonds Database.

At the individual bond level, different innovative financing tools can be used to invest or refinance in energy efficiency and renewable energy systems. One such tool is Property Assessed Clean Energy (PACE) financing. PACE financing allows property owners to invest in energy efficiency upgrades and renewable energy installations for buildings and to repay these investments over 15-20 years via additional annual payments on their property tax bills. PACE financing removes some of the barriers to investment in energy efficiency and renewable energy, namely large upfront capital costs and lack of accurate information (NREL, 2010).

Another innovative mechanism is the Warehouse for Energy Efficiency Loans (WHEEL). Founded in 2014, WHEEL is a public-private partnership that aims to provide homeowners with low-cost financing for residential energy efficiency improvements by creating a secondary market for residential clean energy loans via securitization (Clouse, 2014; Kolstad, 2015). WHEEL purchases and pools small-scale residential energy efficiency loans that are then turned into asset-backed securities. In June 2015, Citi and Renew Financial announced the first securitisation transaction from WHEEL, issuing USD 12.58 million in asset-backed securities backed by pools of unsecured consumer energy efficiency loans (Citigroup, 2015).

References

American Society of Civil Engineers (2014), "America's infrastructure reportcard", www.infrastructurereportcard.org.

Citigroup (2015), "Citi and Renew Financial announce first-ever energy efficiency loan asset-backed security transaction", Press release, 15 June, www.citigroup.com/citi/news/2015/150615a.htm.

Clouse, C.J. (2014), "WHEEL: aligning energy efficiency and securitization", Institutional Investor, 27 May, www.institutionalinvestor.com/article/3345818/asset-management-fixed-income/wheel-aligning-energy-efficiency-and-securitization.html#/.VYsBiBtVhBc.

GEPF (2015), "GEPF chairman's page: GEPF steps up investment in SA's infrastructure", webpage, www.gepf.co.za/index.php/chairmanspage/article/lorem-ipsum3.

GEPF (2012), "Media release", press release, 11 December, www.gepf.co.za/images/pressReleases/Media_Release_--_GEPF_results_presentation_Final.pdf.

Kolstad, L. (2015), "WHEEL's Up for Home Energy Effficiency Loans", Institute for Market Transformation, 6 July, www.imt.org/news/the-current/wheels-up-for-home-energy-efficiency-loans.

NREL (2010), "Fact sheet: Property-Assessed Clean Energy (PACE) financing of renewables and efficiency", National Renewable Energy Laboratory, July, www.nrel.gov/docs/fy10osti/47097.pdf.

NREL (2009), "Fact sheet: Financing public sector projects with clean renewable energy bonds (CREBs)", National Renewable Energy Laboratory, December, www.nrel.gov/docs/fy10osti/46605.pdf.

Soitec (2013), "Soitec completes ZAR 1,000,000,000 inaugural solar financing bond transaction in South Africa", press release, 30 April, www.prnewswire.com/news-releases/soitec-completes-zar-1000000000-inaugural-solar-financing-bond-transaction-in-south-africa-205386281.html.

Annex 1.A2.

Carbon lock-in, stranded assets and hedging climate risk

Infrastructure investments have the ability to "lock-in" future emission levels. Any new investments in fossil fuel infrastructure have implications for the limited carbon budget consistent with avoiding dangerous interference in the climate system. As this budget shrinks and temperatures rise, such investments will eventually force a choice between stranding high-carbon assets "or stranding the planet" (Gurría, 2013).

Investors are finding ways to "decarbonise" their portfolios, to lessen exposure to or to hedge "carbon and climate risk". Under the Montreal Pledge, investors committed to measure and publicly disclose the carbon footprint of their investment portfolios on an annual basis. Following a pledge by members to decarbonise USD 100 billion of institutional equity investment by the 21st Conference of the Parties to the United Nations Framework Convention on Climate (COP21), the Portfolio Decarbonisation Coalition will support the convening of a community of institutional investors measuring and disclosing the carbon footprint of a total of at least USD 500 billion assets.

Issuers, underwriters and others such as the World Bank Group, the HSBC and the Economist (2014) have argued that green bonds are a "natural hedge" for stranded assets and have the potential to offset climate risk exposure in investor portfolios and serve as a destination for capital divested from fossil fuels. As noted in Table 1.4, there is potential to use pure-play, project and asset-backed securities green bonds as instruments to actively hedge against climate policy risks in a portfolio that includes emissions-intensive assets. In practice, the majority of green bonds are secured on the balance sheet of issuers with diversified activities.

The UN-supported Principles for Responsible Investment argues that bonds markets have historically been the "neglected child" of responsible investment, taking a backseat to equities and other asset classes. As of 2016, increasing attention was turning to climate risk, in line with the 2015 G20 Finance Ministers and Central Bank Governors request for the Financial Stability Board "to convene public- and private-sector participants to review how the financial sector can take account of climate-related issues, and the establishment of an industry-led Task Force on Climate-related Financial Disclosures (FSB, 2016).

According to S&P (2015), with climate change and severe weather events garnering rising numbers of headlines, lenders and institutional investors have become more interested in how S&P Ratings Services incorporates environmental and climate risks into its corporate credit ratings, and the impact these risks have had on their ratings. S&P conducted a lookback review of corporate rating actions and surveillance reports and identified 299 cases in which environmental and climate factors either contributed to a rating revision or were a significant factor in their rating analysis. Fifty-six of these cases resulted in a rating action, CreditWatch placement or outlook revision, 44 of which (close to 80%) were negative in direction. The sub-sectors with the greatest exposure to environmental and climate risk thus far have been the oil refining and marketing, regulated utilities, and unregulated power and gas sub-sectors. S&P concludes that as the severity and frequency of environmental and climate risks continue to rise, the numbers of environmental and climate-related corporate rating actions are also expected to accelerate.

References

FSB (2016), *Phase I Report of the Task Force on Climate-Related Financial Disclosures*, Financial Stability Board, Task Force on Climate-Related Financial Disclosures, 31 March, www.fsb-tcfd.org/wp-content/uploads/2016/03/Phase_I_Report_v15.pdf.

Gurría (2013), "The climate challenge: Achieving zero emissions", www.oecd.org/environment/the-climate-challenge-achieving-zero-emissions.htm

S&P (Standard & Poor's Ratings Services) (2015), *How Environmental And Climate Risks Factor Into Global Corporate Ratings*, Standard & Poor's Financial Services, 21 October, https://www.environmental-finance.com/assets/files/How%20Environmental%20And%20Climate%20Risks%20Factor%20Into%20Global%20Corporate%20Ratings%20Oct%2021%202015%20(2).pdf.

The Economist (2014), "Green grow the markets, O", The Economist, 5 July, www.economist.com/news/finance-and-economics/21606326-market-green-bonds-booming-what-makes-bond-green-green-grow.

Chapter 2.

Barriers, policy actions and options for green bond market development and growth

This chapter provides an assessment of barriers to green bond market development and growth, as well as barriers related to: 1) fundamental preconditions for a deep, liquid domestic bond market; and 2) the enabling environment for the development of green infrastructure projects that may be financed or refinanced through the bond markets. The chapter also provides a stock-taking of existing country experiences and actions to overcome barriers to green bond market development. It concludes with a set of policy considerations for fostering sustainable debt capital market access for green infrastructure that emerged from OECD's contributions to the G20 Green Finance Study Group.

Barriers to green bond market development and growth

Introduction

The speed at which green bond markets develop and mature hinges on many variables, including policy and regulatory factors (e.g. policies that create the demand for green projects) and market conditions (e.g. interest rate developments and the credit cycle). These conditions will differ across the jurisdictions in which green bonds have been and will be issued.

Many medium- and long-term green projects with steady cash flows are good candidates for financing by the bond market. However, the bond market, which currently provides about one-third of total financing for corporates globally, has yet to play a comparable role in green financing. The evolving green bond market faces a range of specific challenges and barriers to its further evolution and growth. Policy makers have a number of options available to overcome these barriers and help to grow a sustainable green bond market with integrity. The OECD's modelling scenarios in Chapter 3 suggest that if there is a concerted push by policy makers and market participants to develop the green bond market, it can scale up rapidly to raise and finance the debt capital that will be needed for a transition to a low-carbon economy.

Barriers will differ in importance across jurisdictions. Several challenges are particular to developing and emerging economies, where more fundamental and general actions are needed by governments. For instance, the lack of a domestic debt capital market and other enabling conditions for issuance would need to be addressed in line with longer term financial market development priorities. While this presents a barrier to green bond market growth, it also represents an opportunity for synergy if addressed in tandem with the need for policies more specifically targeted to building a green bond market (CBI/UNEP Inquiry, 2015).

Each country with a bond market will only face a subset of the complete list of barriers that a country starting without a bond market, domestic investor base and framework conditions for long-term investment could face. For any particular emerging green bond market, it is conceivable that a much shorter and more country-specific list of barriers would need to be addressed by policy makers. Accordingly, this chapter aims to provide a comprehensive set of potential barriers that covers a relatively comprehensive set of possible situations at the national level.

Identifying barriers and challenges to scaling green bond markets

This sub-section draws on work undertaken for the G20 Green Finance Study Group by the OECD along with the International Capital Market Association (ICMA), the Climate Bonds Initiative (CBI) and China GFC (OECD et al., 2016) and identifies several challenges to the growth of the green bond market, recognising that their importance may vary for different markets. A detailed list of barriers of green bond-specific issues and broader framework conditions and factors related to the enabling environment for green infrastructure is given in Annex 2.A1.

The selection of these challenges is supported by the results of a Green Finance Study Group (GFSG) survey on "barriers to scaling up the green bond market". The survey received responses from a group of 24 key investors, issuers and intermediaries in the green bond market. According to the survey results, respondents identified the following barriers as being important: "lack of awareness of green bond benefits" (74% of respondents), "lack of local definition of green bonds" (43%), "high cost of meeting green bond requirements" (41%), "lack of ratings, indices and listings (56%), "lack of targeted incentives for green bond issuers" (55%), "difficulties for international investors to access local green bond markets" (67%), and "lack of domestic green investors" (59%).

General challenges to bond market development

Underlying challenges include the underdevelopment of a domestic institutional investor base, the underdevelopment of the credit rating system, a lack of benchmark yield curves, a lack of risk-hedging instruments and insufficient market liquidity. Many of these fundamental challenges, if addressed in a synchronised way, can be immediately beneficial to the development of local currency green bond markets.

Lack of awareness of the benefits of green bonds and existing international guidelines and standards

For some countries, a lack of knowledge of existing international standards is an important barrier. In addition, in some countries there is a lack of understanding of the potential benefits of the green bond market amongst policy makers, regulators, as well as potential bond issuers and investors. Some finance professionals may simply not have heard of green bonds. In these cases global green bond market participants, for example supranational organisations and multilateral development banks (MDBs), can communicate the benefits of green bonds to these various groups.

Lack of local green bond guidelines

For a variety of reasons, countries may need to develop their local currency green bond markets. For example, in countries where capital investment is not fully open, the local green bond markets will rely on local investors. In some countries, the priorities of their environmental challenges (e.g. air and water pollution being the top priorities) are somewhat different from other countries that focus on controlling greenhouse gas emissions, such as the case is in the People's Republic of China (hereafter "China") with regards to air pollution. In such countries policy incentives may be used to support the local green bond market. In some of these markets they may require additional definitions and disclosure than the Green Bond Principles require for particular categories. For these countries, the first barrier is the lack of local definitions and disclosure requirements for green bonds.

This barrier may also be relevant in other circumstances, e.g. in countries where capital investment is not fully open and where local green bond markets will rely on local investors.

Costs of meeting green bond requirements

The verification of the "green bond" status and the monitoring of use of proceeds by issuers for green purposes are performed mainly by second-opinion or third-party assurance providers (such as accountancy firms and specialised research agencies). However, many potential issuers still do not have the knowledge of how such a verification process may work. In some markets, the relatively high cost of obtaining a second-opinion or third-party assurance (ranging from USD 10 000 to USD 100 000) is also a barrier for some small issuers. Some issuers have also complained about the high costs of managing disclosure requirements.

Lack of green bond ratings, indices and listings

Green credit ratings, which incorporate environmental information in the ratings of the bonds, can help the market evaluate the alignment of green bonds with international guidelines and standards such as the Green Bond Principles (GBP) and the Climate Bonds Initiative (CBI) standard, and may also help investors understand the impact of environmental factors in the overall risk profile of issuers. Green bond indices can guide bond investors to invest in green bonds that meet their criteria. This can result in increased fund flows that can also help reduce funding costs for green issuers. Green bond listing criteria implemented by stock exchanges can have similar benefits. However, currently, only a relatively small number of rating agencies, index companies and stock exchanges have promoted such green products and policies.

Lack of supply of labelled green bonds

In some markets, investor appetite for green bonds is relatively strong, as evidenced by significant oversubscriptions of recent issuances. For such markets, the lack of supply of "labelled" green bonds is a major constraint. At a higher level this reflects the lack of bankable green projects in some markets that can be financed or refinanced through green bonds. This focuses attention on the need to foster robust enabling policy environments necessary for pipelines of green projects to emerge at scale. In addition to the lack of issuance of bonds whose proceeds are spent on green projects, there is also the issue of the relatively low share of potentially qualifying bonds that are actually labelled as "green". The number of bonds that meet one of the existing standards (ICMA, CBI or China's definitions) and could potentially qualify for a green label could be many times larger than the number of "green bonds" that are already labelled as such.

Difficulties for international investors to access local markets

While global green investors exist, they sometimes find it difficult to access certain local markets. One problem here is that green bond definitions and disclosure requirements differ across markets. These differences increase transaction costs as bonds recognised as green in one market need to be relabelled or recertified in another market. Another barrier to cross-border green bond investing is the lack of risk-hedging products (e.g. against currency risks).

Lack of domestic green investors

In markets where green bonds are mostly bought by local investors due either to capital controls or definitional barriers, the existence of institutional investors that have a preference for green assets is important to ensure there is sufficient demand. However, due to factors such as the lack of disclosure requirements for institutional investors to reveal environmental information of their asset holdings and the lack of capacity to quantify the environmental costs and benefits of their investments, many investors do not have the tools (including indices) to distinguish between green and non-green assets in the domestic bond market.

The risks, perceived and real, of green bonds

Green bond investors wish to see reductions in risk at the market, project and creditor levels. While institutional investors have driven the growth in the market so far, they prefer commoditised investment products that deliver risk-adjusted returns, with low due diligence costs. Their appetite to invest in green bonds likely will increase over time as projects and markets mature, moving from left to right in Figure 2.1. As markets mature, the volume and liquidity of debt will increase, reducing volatility, reducing uncertainty in performance and reducing issuance costs through standardisation.

In order for the green bond market to reach sufficient scale, a significant portion of the underlying assets will have to achieve mature status. Large-scale "commoditised" finance requires a high proportion of assets to reach stage 4, that is, to be operating at scale, with standardisation and pooling, credit rating agency "surveillance", and availability of historical data with correspondingly low technological and market risks. In the transition to 2035, there will be a role for policy makers to play to ensure that policy risks are mitigated and market barriers overcome.[1]

At a more granular level, as projects move from development through to operation, and establish a track record, their risks decline and they become more suitable as collateral for securities as well as more attractive to the deeper pools of capital with lower risk appetites (i.e. institutional investors). Not shown in the figure are the changes to the credit risk of the issuer over time. Currently, green corporate and supranational, sub-sovereign and agency (SSA) bond investors are rarely materially exposed to policy or technology risk because most green bonds issued today provide direct recourse to the balance sheet of the issuer in the case of default, rather than the project. This could change significantly in the future as more project bonds and asset-backed securities are issued, exposing investors directly to project-level risk and commensurate risk-adjusted return. More pure-play corporates specialising in new, green assets may emerge as these sectors grow and generate more visible cash flows that can support debt issuance in public markets, and their green debt will be more closely associated with policy or technology risk.

Figure 2.1. **The phases of green infrastructure asset development at individual and market level**

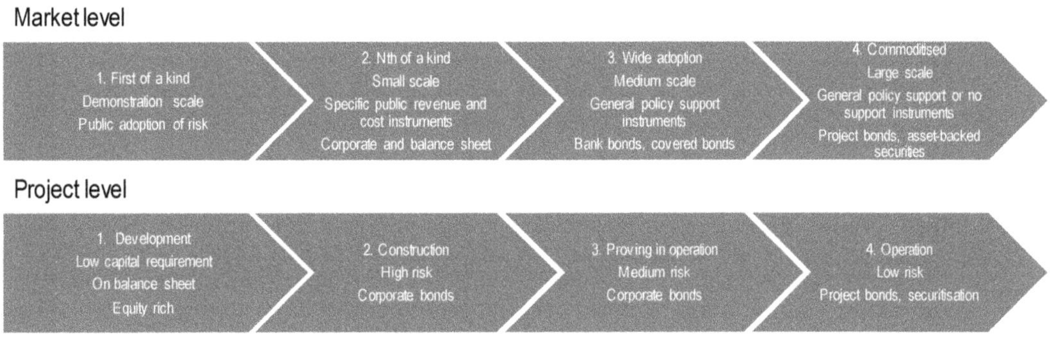

Country experiences and actions to overcome barriers to green bond market development

Since the emergence of the green bond market, governments and public financial institutions have moved to address barriers specifically related to green bonds through a variety of actions and approaches. Government actions that are undertaken as part of broader objectives to develop financial markets have the effect of establishing preconditions for (green) bond issuance. These preconditions include the need for robust domestic capital markets,[2] the presence of institutional investors with the capacity to invest in green bonds[3] and a broader enabling environment for green infrastructure investment.[4] Due to differences in local conditions, some options that are considered as good practices in one country may not be suitable for another country. This chapter therefore has focused on stocktaking, knowledge sharing, and developing voluntary options for countries to choose from and for bilateral and multilateral collaboration.

If these elements are in place, bankable pipelines of projects that can be financed and refinanced through green bonds can emerge. To date, green bond-specific actions have been taken either after preconditions for a domestic bond market have been met, or simultaneously with actions to put these preconditions in place. Actions specific to green bonds are geared at building the market and stimulating the demand or supply side of the green bond market. They can take the form of government and public financial institution intervention at the project level (e.g. risk mitigation) or at the securities market level (e.g. tax support). A more in-depth examination of issues related to developing local currency bond markets (LCBMs) and mobilising institutional investors is included in Annex 2.A2.

Building the market

1. Governments are supporting the development and harmonisation of guidelines and definitions for green bonds. Such efforts are taking place in China through the People's Bank of China (PBoC) and in India through the Securities and Exchange Board (SEBI). France has established a green label for investment funds that is aligned with the Green Bond Principles (under the auspices of its Energy Transition Law),[5] and at the EU level, supporting green bond finance through convergence of green bond standards based on market-led initiatives is on the EU's policy agenda under the Capital Markets Union. A group of 11 public financial institutions agreed on a harmonised framework for impact reporting on projects to which green bond proceeds have been allocated.[6]
2. Countries are active in setting the enabling environment for aggregation and green securitisation. The European Central Bank runs a loan data depository and public green investment banks in the United States are warehousing green loans.[7] The US Department of Energy and its National Renewable Energy Laboratory (NREL) backed a solar securitisation initiative (Solar Access to Public Capital) that is now being extended to China (the Chinese PV Alliance) and Europe (RESFARM). In Mexico, a demonstration green securitisation programme for energy efficiency is currently underway, supported by the Inter-American Development Bank.
3. Legal changes can also support the emergence of green bonds. Germany had its first green covered bond issuance after it extended its dedicated legal framework for covered bond issuances to green projects. In the United States, the establishment of Property Assessed Clean Energy (PACE) bond legislation enables municipalities to raise money for energy-saving retrofits for households and businesses.
4. As of August 2015, half of G20 countries had a national infrastructure plan and some (less than a third) had a pipeline.[8] The Canadian province of Ontario has taken the further step of linking its pipeline of green projects to its municipal green bond programme.[9]

Demand-side policies

1. Public green bond investment mandates. Norway's Sovereign Wealth Fund invests in green bonds, as do multiple public pension funds (including in South Africa, Sweden and California), the Bangladeshi central bank and the UN Joint

Staff Pension Fund.[10] Germany's national development bank, KfW, invests in green bonds on behalf of the German government. Cornerstone investments are also possible for inaugural green bonds as was done by the International Finance Corporation (IFC) for an Indian green bond (issued by Yes Bank) and by Australia's public green investment bank (Clean Energy Finance Corporation) for a local financial sector green bond (issued by National Australia Bank).

2. National green bond market development committees. These arrangements are being set up in seven G20 countries to co-ordinate among key stakeholders such as finance ministries, public issuers and investors.[11] A working group has also been established to promote and develop Shari'ah-compliant financial products (including Green Sukuk) in Islamic jurisdictions to invest in climate change solutions.[12]

Supply-side policies

1. Public sector "demonstration issuance" of green bonds. Public entities can issue green bonds in line with their fiscal and debt management parameters. MDBs have been the pioneering and leading issuers. National development banks such as KfW, Export-Import Banks in Korea and India, and export credit agencies in Canada and Sweden are all active issuers, as well as municipalities and local funding authorities in five G20 countries.[13] Hawaii's green investment bank capitalised itself through green bond issuance.[14] These public sector sources (i.e. SSA and municipal issuers) were responsible for almost half of green bond issuance in 2015. After introducing guidelines for socially responsible debt, Malaysia's state-owned sovereign wealth fund (Khazanah Nasional Berhad) issued Green Sukuk.
2. Issuer advice. The IFC is also starting to advise potential private green bond issuers in emerging markets on aligning with the GBPs.
3. Governments have provided risk mitigation, credit enhancement and other public intervention in support of green bonds where they deem this support appropriate. The US government's development finance institution, OPIC, offers "green guaranties". One such guarantee is currently supporting a Chilean solar PV project, which when complete will be the largest such project in Latin America. At a regional level the EU/EIB Project Bond Credit Enhancement Initiative provided a credit enhancement for a green project bond backing an off-shore wind interconnector, which also attracted investment from a Danish pension fund.[15]
4. Tax incentives. Many governments exempt municipal bond issuances from tax.[16] For example, the United States has a tax exemption for municipal issuances where interest and coupons can be tax-free at federal or state levels. In addition, the United States has offered special tax incentives for bonds financing green buildings as well as renewable energy through the Clean Renewable Energy Bond and Qualified Energy Conservation Bond programmes.

Emerging options and policy considerations for mobilising the bond markets for green infrastructure

This section proposes a set of policy considerations for fostering access to the bond markets for green infrastructure. In line with the G20 "Green finance synthesis report" (G20, 2016), this section discusses options that draw on current actions that are being taken, that the public, official and private sectors can consider on a voluntary basis. It is informed in part by the emerging options discussed in the "Green finance synthesis report" and in OECD et al. (2016), which can be referred to for further context and explanation.

The diversity that characterises the green and low-carbon bond financing channel means that a wide range of policies can play a useful role, if they are tailored to the specific facts and circumstances in a country and sector (e.g. bond sector or underlying asset sector) and with regard to new technologies that become more available for deployment and bond financing over time (such as solar thermal, energy storage, carbon capture and storage, bio-sequestration and other green innovations yet to be commercialised or even invented).

Preconditions exist for the emergence of the green assets that can be financed or refinanced through green bonds and for mobilising institutional investor participation in the green bond market. These are discussed in Annex 2.A2 with respect to fundamental bond market development activities, and provided in abridged form below (these preconditions are covered in depth in OECD [2015b]; G20/OECD [2015], [2014]; and IMF et al. [2013]).

Preconditions

1. Establish an enabling environment. For bond issuance and for institutional investors to provide long-term investment financing (see G20/OECD, 2013; 2014). This includes taking steps to: 1) improve the business climate, rule of law and investment regime underpinning sustainable infrastructure investments; 2) strengthen competition policy and level the playing field between the private sector and state-owned enterprises.
2. Ensure a stable, transparent and integrated "investment-grade" policy environment for green investment. Institute a "green investment policy framework" with cost-effective support policies where appropriate (see OECD, 2015a, 2015b, 2015c; Corfee-Morlot et al., 2012); avoid sudden or retroactive change to support policies in order to provide predictability to investors; examine the case for introducing barriers to policy change through legislation or contractual liabilities that make it unattractive to change policies retrospectively. Put an explicit price on carbon and phase out fossil fuel subsidies; provide an electricity market context that assures a reasonable and predictable return for investors in low-carbon power generation and associated enabling infrastructure. Promote and harmonise well-designed and time-bound renewable energy support policies, when needed, to improve risk-return profiles. Promote the use of contracts such as power purchase agreements that provide the stable and certain cash flows.
3. Apart from these, government and the official sector can consider a further range of policy measures that may be warranted, in various areas as listed in the following in terms of general policy considerations (G20/OECD, 2015).

Regulation

1. Design and oversight. Careful design and oversight of markets for green bonds and securitised asset-backed securities (ABS) in particular, can help to foster the use of alternative financing instruments and provide an avenue for capital

recycling, without putting at stake the overall resilience of the financial system (see Nassr and Wehinger, 2015; G20/OECD, 2015).

2. Regulatory approach. Sensible and balanced calibration [17] of the existing regulatory frameworks affecting different types of green bonds (e.g. covered, ABS, corporate, etc.) should be pursued, particularly given the potential role of institutional investors in providing alternative sources of debt financing (G20/OECD, 2015). Regulation should also take a holistic and co-ordinated approach to avoid regulatory arbitrage, in which investors favour specific instruments over others due to differences in regulatory treatment. A co-ordinated regulatory approach would avoid unduly favouring specific instruments over others with similar characteristics and creating associated distortions in risk pricing. Healthy competition should be secured across similar financing solutions, eliminating any imbalances or disincentives that might direct investor and issuer preferences away from some of these instruments (see G20/OECD, 2015).
3. Create specific market frameworks. Creating regulatory and legislative frameworks for specific asset classes such as ABS and project bonds (e.g. in the United States and the European Union), covered bonds (e.g. in Germany) and private placement bonds (e.g. in the United States and the European Union) at national or broader international levels can open up these green bond channels. Such securities should have an investment horizon in line with those of the underlying assets and should be developed in co-operation with institutional investors.

Market building

1. Identify project pipeline. The amount of green bonds that can be issued will be determined by market demand and the availability of suitable greenfield and brownfield projects that can be financed or refinanced through the bond markets. China and India have developed pipelines for infrastructure, and Kenya has published a strategic project priority list. The Canadian province of Ontario has linked a pipeline of green projects to its municipal green bond programme. National agencies for infrastructure have been established in Australia, South Africa and the United Kingdom which can co-ordinate and deploy these types of project pipeline plans. Governments can benefit from working more closely with development banks and investors in this process, who also maintain project pipelines for their green bond issuance programmes.
2. Develop green guidelines and standards. Scientifically rigorous standards, guidelines and procedures for verification can allow for straightforward certification and issuance of bond instruments that verifiably contribute to a low-carbon economy, leading to increased market transparency, comparability and market integrity. Additionally, they can help prevent the risk of so-called "greenwashing" whereby proceeds from bonds issued do not actually contribute to the intended projects or corporate activities. Green bonds have developed to date largely thanks to market-led initiatives that have produced international guidelines and standards represented in particular by the GBP and the CBI Standard that aim to promote and protect the integrity of the green bond market. These guidelines and standards may be market-led or developed by governments. Governments can support the development, adoption and harmonisation of emerging certification standards for green bonds such as the Climate Bond

Standard and Certification Scheme and voluntary guidelines such as the Green Bond Principles. As a result, they have been recognised by the official sector and have served as a key reference for countries such as China and India that have developed Green Bond Guidelines and definitions to guide the local market, as well as an official evaluation system to ensure that issuers adhere to the guidelines. Further efforts to more firmly anchor the market's "green" credibility, such as defining international rules, could address uncertainties in the market that could jeopardise its growth, and could help overcome many of the barriers identified earlier in this chapter.

3. Providing technical assistance for developing local green bond guidelines. As previously described, due to reasons ranging from capital controls to domestic environmental considerations and other policy preferences, some countries may choose to develop their local currency green bond markets. In these cases, it is important that international lessons and experiences are made available and fully studied when developing their local green bond definitions, taxonomies and disclosure requirements. International organisations with green finance specialisation or capabilities should assist in capacity building for the drafting of key documents as the basis for operating the local currency green bond markets. The objective of local green bond standards should be to ensure that while the national agenda is met, these local green bond rules do not create unnecessary barriers to or transaction costs for cross-border green capital flows. Local currency green bond taxonomies should reflect where necessary the country's demands for combating its domestic environmental challenges, while remaining as consistent as possible with international guidelines and standards (such as the GBP and the CBI Standard). They should also be simple enough to enable most market actors, who are not specialists in the environmental areas, to comprehend. In such cases where taxonomies will be used by authorities or regulators to approve green bond issuance and to grant favourable policy support (such as interest subsidies and guarantees), these definitions need to be sufficiently specific so that they can form the basis for decision making.

4. Raising international awareness of the benefits of green bonds. A key lever for green bond market development is effective market education on the benefits of green bonds (for sustainable development, for issuers, and for investors) as well as the awareness of international green bond standards and disclosure requirements. Promotional efforts can be organised by government agencies, regulators, market associations, financial institutions, development agencies, rating agencies, second-opinion and third-party assurance providers. MDBs and international organisations with a mandate for sustainable investment can also organise dissemination events in countries that they cover.

5. Centralised data depositories. As a precursor to aggregation and securitisation, governments can start and provide support to initiatives that aim to build up loan-level data, performance track records, definitions and second-party verifications. For instance the European Central Bank set up the European DataWarehouse depository in 2013 for loans underlying European ABS. Pooling this type of data in centralised depositories, set up and maintained through public initiatives, should benefit the functioning and liquidity of the entire green infrastructure financing market through increasing transparency. This will in turn allow for informed decision making by capital holders while facilitating monitoring by supervisors, reducing information asymmetries and reducing

transaction costs associated with due diligence. Appropriate balance in the level of disclosure requirements should nonetheless be safeguarded so as to stimulate investor appetite through transparency without rendering such issuance or investment overly costly or cumbersome.

6. Aggregation. Securitisation is one option to aggregate small-scale green projects to be suitable for green bond issuance. In Mexico, a deal aggregating energy efficiency loans and providing demonstration of green securitisations is currently underway, supported by the Inter-American Development Bank. In the United States, the National Renewable Energy Laboratory (NREL) of the Department of Energy has set up a solar securitisation working group that includes industry actors. Public institutions could also set up a green project warehouse (which includes data as well as the loans themselves) to aggregate small-scale assets across originating entities. In the United States, the state of Pennsylvania has established a Warehouse for Energy Efficiency loans in collaboration with the commercial bank Citi.

7. Version standardisation. The development of standardised "off-the-shelf" versions of green bonds (e.g. for municipalities) and ABS could be pursued with a view to lowering the transaction costs and increasing the efficiency and accessibility of green bonds to issuers and investors. For example, the Basel Committee on Banking Supervision and the International Organization of Securities Commissions created criteria for identifying simple, transparent and comparable securitisations. Support for the creation of indices could be envisaged to enhance liquidity and investor participation in publicly traded green bonds.

8. Technical assistance for local currency bond market development. Technical assistance for developing local currency bond markets in areas such as the development of benchmark yield curves, ratings, risk mitigation mechanisms and FX hedging products can also be helpful for growing the green bond market. Such efforts should occur in collaboration with any green bond market participants already active in a country. As a considerable amount of the green bond market's growth has occurred as a result of private sector development and innovation, governments should work to support such efforts.

9. Developing green bond indices, ratings and stock exchange lists. Index companies and other financial institutions can develop green bond indices as a basis for green bond ETFs and other fund products. Rating agencies could further develop or acquire the technical expertise needed to launch green bond ratings that cover the full spectrum of bonds. Securities exchanges could consider green bond listings as a future business driver. International organisations, public research institutions and non-governmental organisations can provide further support group share tools and systems to make it easier (and less costly) for issuers to manage their green assets, and for second-opinion providers, rating companies and index companies to assess the green impact of the bond-financed projects. These include various analytical tools (such as open source solutions for quantifying the environmental benefits, e.g. emission reductions, energy savings and water savings) and related reporting tools (such as data aggregators that reduce the reporting cost of individual institutions).

Demand side

1. Strategic public green bond investment mandates. Sovereign wealth funds and public pension funds are well placed to invest in green bonds, playing a demonstration role for private sector investors. Green bonds can represent a form of investment that yields long-term, stable returns that may suit the public mandates of sovereign wealth funds and public pension funds. Public investors can collaborate with governments to grow the green bond market. For instance, the German national development bank KfW has been authorised to act as an "anchor investor" in a EUR 1 billion portfolio of green bonds on behalf of the German government, backed by the Federal Ministry for the Environment, Nature Conservation, Building and Nuclear Safety (BMUB) which jointly with KfW defines a "minimum quality requirement" for green bonds that are eligible for the portfolio. This type of collaboration promotes the quality-based development of the green bonds market by focusing public demand on green bonds that meet certain standards of transparency in use of proceeds and impact reporting.[18] Brazil's BNDES state development bank is another example of a public entity that supports green bonds. Cornerstone investment from public financial institutions can also strengthen the market by reducing perceived risk for private investors. The IFC has, for example, invested in green bonds issued by Indian Yes Bank, using funds raised by its own IFC green bond issuance in the offshore rupee markets.
2. Incubating local green investors. For markets that rely mostly on local investors, efforts can be made to "incubate" domestic green institutional investors, via building capacity for them to identify green assets, to improve the transparency of holdings and to adopt environment, social and governance (ESG) principles in investment decision making. Steps that can help incubate a local green investor base include: strong government signals in support of green investment; green finance associations that help raise awareness and provide training for green investment practices; encouragement for institutional investors to examine the environmental performance of their asset holdings; and international collaboration on capacity building.
3. Collaboration. One collaborative model that has emerged in the market is national green bond market development committees representing various stakeholders, in particular financial regulators, ministries of finance and development banks. Committees are currently being organised in Brazil, Canada, China, India, Mexico and Turkey. Global co-operation between the committees will allow ideas and policy proposals to be shared and activities to be synchronised.
4. Promoting international collaboration to facilitate cross-border green capital flows. Different markets could collaborate to facilitate the harmonisation of definitions and verification process of green bonds and the development of green asset-backed securities acceptable by foreign investors. These efforts can take the form of bilateral collaboration between markets, to demonstrate their effect of enhancing cross-border green bond investment flows.

Supply side

1. Public sector demonstration issuance. Public entities can issue green bonds in line with their fiscal parameters and criteria and priorities for lending and bond issuance. Public financial institutions and MDBs have been pioneering and

leading issuers of green bonds, led by the European Investment Bank and the World Bank Group. National development banks and public green investment banks have also issued green bonds. Public export-import banks, export credit agencies and municipality-linked public entities have issued green bonds.

2. Technical assistance for investors. Governments can incentivise and support the deployment of appropriate internal institutional infrastructures (due diligence capacity, models, monitoring systems), which could create efficiencies in investors' due diligence and other procedures and facilitate their participation in a green asset-backed securities market. This is underway for securitisations more generally under certain financial regulations.
3. Reducing the costs of green bond issuance and reporting. Standardisation of methodologies, as GBP is doing with reporting templates and CBI with green definitions, is designed to lower the cost and effort of verification. Governments, international organisations and non governmental organisations can sponsor the development and dissemination of tools to support cost-effective analysis of the environmental benefits of green bond-supported projects. Such efforts can contribute to mitigating global market inefficiencies whereby environmental benefits are not adequately priced. The public sector and MDBs could also consider measures to reduce the costs of green bond verification in early-stage markets (e.g. by covering part of the costs). The IFC has already indicated it is exploring measures to do this in relation to commercial bank green bond issuance in emerging markets.
4. Labelling qualified "green bonds". For bonds that qualify as "green" but are not yet self-labelled or verified by third-party assurance, financial service providers and non-governmental organisations can consider labelling them as "green bonds". Subject to being consistent with accepted practice for new green bonds such as the GBP and the Climate Bonds Standard, such a labelling exercise can substantially increase the availability of green assets, thereby easing supply-side constraints on some markets.

Public intervention

1. Risk mitigation. Consistent with broader policy, governments can provide risk mitigation and other public intervention in support of green bonds where this would result in more appropriate allocation of risks and their associated returns. Governments may use public financing mechanisms to provide cover for risks that are new to investors and cannot be covered in existing markets. Such mechanisms may include, *inter alia*, insurance-related options, credit enhancement tools, guarantees and tax options (G20/OECD, 2013; 2014).
2. Public intervention design. Design should be decided on the basis of identified market failures, and should be selected by carrying out appropriate cost-benefit analysis of such interventions and ensuring that any public support is appropriately priced and is subject to fiscal considerations. Risk mitigants should be designed on a case-by-case basis, according to market best practices, and in such a way that private sector participation is not crowded out. Specific evaluation and control procedures (beyond a standard impact assessment) would need to be put in place to ensure that the intended (capital, funding) benefit is passed on to the real economy. Some governments do not offer risk mitigation as a matter of public policy, given the risks entailed, which can include potential

price and competitive distortions as well as rising contingent liabilities and other budgetary problems. Public financial institutions and development banks can facilitate risk mitigation for green bonds and to the projects underlying green bonds, by providing coverage for government-related, sovereign risks, as well as for specific operational risks including regulatory changes and currency exposure (G20/OECD, 2013; 2015).

3. Financial stability oversight. While the size of the green securitisation market is small in terms of the wider financial system, it has the potential to grow significantly. Therefore, careful assessment of the riskiness of inappropriate design and use of such instruments should be encouraged in the context of a widely interconnected financial system. The corresponding benefits to the real economy and their materiality to green corporates and projects should be part of such an assessment (G20/OECD, 2013; 2015).
4. Dialogue. Official support for raising the profile of the public debate on green bond initiatives may help to overcome the barriers to green bond market development identified and encourage the appropriate and safe use of financing instruments such as ABS.

Emerging from the list of options and considerations is a general need to enhance the role of MDBs/development financial institutions (DFIs) and public entities in developing green bond markets. One of the low-cost approaches to developing the green bond market, and leveraging the substantial experiences that have been accumulated by many MDBs, DFIs and public sector entities (such as local governments), is to have them play a more important role in green bond market development.

Through developing green bond markets, MDBs and DFIs can also kick-start the overall growth of a country's bond market. For example, credit enhancement for municipal green bonds can grow a local municipal bond market more broadly. The growth of India's bond market in response to public sector support for infrastructure bond issuance is an example of such an effect. Possible areas drawn from the previous list that MDBs and DFIs can contribute to significantly include:

- demonstration issuance, including issuance in local currency green bond markets
- providing credit enhancements (such as the IFC's green bond guarantee programme)
- providing analytics and tools for environmental impact analysis for green bond-supported projects
- setting up vehicles to aggregate investor demand for emerging markets green bonds
- serving as an anchor investor for green bonds.

Assessing the effectiveness of policy measures

Assessing the effectiveness of policy measures to advance the green bond market is challenging. The scale of funds flowing through the channel is not a reliable measure of the incremental contribution of green bond-specific policies. Many other policies contribute to the flow, and many other channels also serve green investments.

Keys to evaluating policies for the green bond market may include cost-benefit analysis approaches including an examination of whether green bonds are lowering the cost of capital for green projects, and whether they lower the total social cost of matching investors with investments, thereby incrementally increasing the flow of funds to green investments. Given green infrastructure investments are capital intensive, even small changes in the weighted average cost of capital can significantly improve the levelised costs of green infrastructure compared to carbon-intensive alternatives, and can strengthen the fundamentals for increased deployment. Recent history shows many ways in which green bond policies have been effective in lowering costs and expanding the flow of capital to green infrastructure. More work is needed in this area to develop and define metrics for evaluating green bond policies as the market grows and matures.

Policy will have to evolve and respond to a changing context. As the economy grows and changes, as new information and understanding of the climate change challenge develops, as international negotiations take new turns, all governments must adapt their policies accordingly. New green bond policies will be needed in the near future as well, as new types of projects become commercial and available for deployment at scale.

Notes

1. In any scenario with large-scale asset securitisation, policy makers should also be able to consider any adverse effects at a systemic level of policy reversals, and problems with the underlying assets that only become apparent over time (e.g. technological failures).

2. Governments address these issues in line with longer term financial market development priorities. For instance, since 2011, the OECD has been working with the IMF, the World Bank and others on the G20 Action Plan to support the development of local currency bond markets, which could also be applied to green bonds.

3. See for instance the "G20/OECD checklist and report on effective approaches to support implementation of the G20/OECD high-level principles on long-term investment financing by institutional investors" (G20/OECD, 2014).

4. These include carbon pricing, fossil fuel subsidy removal and reform and a transparent, stable and credible policy framework for supporting green infrastructure. For more details see for instance the OECD's "Policy Guidance for Investment in Clean Energy", the "Policy Framework for Investment", and the "Green Investment Policy Framework" (OECD, 2015c).

5. www.developpement-durable.gouv.fr/Energy-and-Ecological-Transition.html.

6. See ICMA (2015).

7. In 2014, the Connecticut Green Bank established a USD 40 million facility for construction-phase lending and loan aggregation for commercial and industrial energy efficiency and renewable energy investments which are sold off to institutional investors, supporting the operational phase.

8. Infrastructure plan: Australia, Canada, China, Italy, Korea, Mexico, South Africa, Spain, Turkey, the United Kingdom and the United States. Infrastructure project pipeline: Australia, Brazil, the EU, France, Italy and Mexico (G20/OECD, 2015).

9. The Province of Ontario has formed a Green Bond Advisory Panel, which includes staff from various ministries and agencies, including the Ministry of the Environment and Climate Change and the Ontario Financing Authority. The panel screens and selects projects for use of proceeds that align with Ontario's environmental and climate change policies and pipeline of projects. In October 2014, Ontario successfully launched a Green Bond programme with an inaugural green bond of CAD 500 million. In January 2016, Ontario issued its second green bond, raising CAD 750 million to support low-carbon infrastructure projects. Source: www.ofina.on.ca/greenbonds/greenbonds.htm.

10. South Africa (Government Employees Pension Fund); Sweden (AP2 and AP3); California (CalSTRS and CalPERS).

11. Brazil, Canada, China, India, Mexico, Turkey and California.

12. Green Sukuk and Working Party (GSWP) established by the MENA Clean Energy Business Council, the Climate Bonds Initiative, and the Gulf Bond and Sukuk Association (GBSA).

13. France, Norway, South Africa, Sweden and the United States.

14. Responding to the need to make private rooftop solar photovoltaic more accessible, Hawaii's Green Energy Market Securitization programme (GEMS) was designed in 2013 to increase the availability of financing. GEMS issued USD 150 million in green bonds to fully fund its initial capitalisation. The bond will be repaid using funds from an existing consumer surcharge on electrical bills. The GEMS "green bonds" received an award (the 2014 International Financing Review North America Structured Finance Issue Award) in recognition of the innovation of using a rate-reduction bond structure to finance renewable energy infrastructure.

15. The Greater Gabbard offshore transmission link has become the first UK-based infrastructure project to attract finance from institutional investors using the Project Bond Credit Enhancement initiative.

16. For instance, the United States provides tax incentives to more than 80% of the USD 3.7 trillion municipal bond market. Interest on US municipal bonds is exempt from federal income tax. Bond coupons are usually exempt from state tax as well. Brazil allows tax-free bonds to be issued for large infrastructure investments, construction conglomerates and wind farm developers.

17. See Nassr and Wehinger (2015) for further explanation.

18. See KfW (2015).

References

CBI/UNEP Inquiry (2015), "Scaling green bond markets for sustainable development", Climate Bonds Initiative and United Nations Environment Programme, September, https://www.climatebonds.net/files/files/CBI-Guide-2015-final-web.pdf.

Corfee-Morlot, J. et al. (2012), "Towards a green investment policy framework: The case of low-carbon, climate-resilient infrastructure", *OECD Environment Working Papers*, No. 48, OECD Publishing, Paris, http://dx.doi.org/10.1787/5k8zth7s6s6d-en.

G20 (2016), "G20 green finance synthesis report", G20 Green Finance Study Group, 5 September, http://unepinquiry.org/wp-content/uploads/2016/09/Synthesis_Report_Full_EN.pdf.

G20/OECD (2015), "Progress report on G20/OECD high-level principles on SME financing", OECD Report to G20 Finance Ministers and Central Bank Governors, September, OECD, Paris, www.oecd.org/g20/topics/financing-for-investment/G20-OECD-High-level-Principles-on-SME-Financing-Progress-Report.pdf.

G20/OECD (2014), "G20/OECD report on effective approaches to support implementation of the G20/OECD high-level principles on long-term investment financing by institutional investors", Report to G20 Finance Ministers and Central Bank Governors, September, OECD, Paris, www.oecd.org/daf/fin/private-pensions/G20-OECD-Report-Effective-Approaches-LTI-Financing-Sept-2014.pdf.

G20/OECD (2013), "G20/OECD high-level principles of long-term investment financing by institutional investors", September, OECD, Paris, www.oecd.org/daf/fin/private-pensions/G20-OECD-Principles-LTI-Financing.pdf.

ICMA (2015), "Green bonds: Working towards a harmonized framework for impact reporting", International Capital Market Association, December, www.icmagroup.org/assets/documents/Regulatory/Green-Bonds/20151202-0530-FINALRevised-Proposal.pdf.

IMF et al. (2013), "Local currency bond markets: A diagnostic framework", International Monetary Fund, Washington, DC, 9 July, www.oecd.org/daf/fin/public-debt/Local-Currency-Bond-Markets-Diagnostic-Framework-2013.pdf.

KfW (2015), "KfW promotes climate protection with purchase of green bonds: Planned portfolio in the amount of EUR 1 billion", press release, 4 September, https://www.kfw.de/KfW-Group/Newsroom/Aktuelles/Pressemitteilungen/Pressemitteilungen-Details_269248.html.

Nassr, I.K. and G. Wehinger (2015), "Unlocking SME finance through market-based debt: Securitisation, private placements and bonds", *OECD Journal: Financial Market Trends*, Vol. 2014(2), OECD Publishing Paris, http://dx.doi.org/10.1787/fmt-2014-5js3bg1g53ln.

OECD (2015a), *Aligning Policies for a Low-carbon Economy*, OECD Publishing, Paris, http://dx.doi.org/10.1787/9789264233294-en.

OECD (2015b), *Mapping Channels to Mobilise Institutional Investment in Sustainable Energy*, Green Finance and Investment, OECD Publishing, Paris, http://dx.doi.org/10.1787/9789264224582-en.

OECD (2015c), *Policy Guidance for Investment in Clean Energy Infrastructure: Expanding Access to Clean Energy for Green Growth and Development*, OECD Publishing, Paris, http://dx.doi.org/10.1787/9789264212664-en.

OECD et al. (2016) "Green bonds: Country experiences, barriers and options", OECD/ICMA/CBI/China GFC, http://unepinquiry.org/wp-content/uploads/2016/09/6_Green_Bonds_Country_Experiences_Barriers_and_Options.pdf.

Annex 2.A1.

Barriers related to bond market preconditions and enabling environment for green infrastructure investment

Each country with a bond market will only face a subset of the complete list of barriers that a country starting without a bond market, domestic investor base and framework conditions for long-term investment could face. For any particular emerging green bond market, it is conceivable that a much shorter and more country-specific list of barriers would need to be addressed by policy makers. Accordingly, this report aims to provide a comprehensive set of potential barriers that covers a relatively comprehensive set of possible situations at the national level.

Table 2.A1.1. **Barriers related to framework conditions and enabling environment for green infrastructure**

BARRIER
1. Enabling environment: Preconditions, macro and market factors
1.1. Macroeconomic, political and business climate
Absence of stable macroeconomic conditions and political environment preclude progress on other preconditions for bond issuance
Unfavourable business and investment climate, inconsistent and ineffective enforcement of the rule of law, insufficient and unreliable creditor rights and insolvency regimes, especially those underpinning green investments
1.2. Local currency bond market (LCBM)
1.2.1. Lack of: a suitable issuance framework for a wholesale market; a credible credit rating framework; adequate trading, clearing and settlement systems; a long-term government yield curve and pricing benchmarks
1.2.2. Lack of: robust securitisation frameworks, including flexible special-purpose vehicles; and a robust public-private partnership framework
1.2.3. Absence of a credible regulator with knowledge and capabilities to oversee the market
1.3. Regulation
1.3.1. Calibration of existing financial sector regulatory and taxation frameworks for different types of bonds not holistic and co-ordinated, leading to investor preference for other types of bonds or investments
1.4. Investor base
1.4.1. Lack of or underdeveloped national savings mobilisation vehicles and policies, long-term savings and domestic institutional investors
1.5. Interest rates
1.5.1. Interest rate policy and stability that negatively affects the overall attractiveness of debt financing and creates specific biases against green bond instruments[1]
1.6. Market conditions
1.6.1. Insufficient number of credit market actors and corresponding market illiquidity that restricts green bond market formation and development
1.6.2. Energy markets: Low prices on fossil fuels that, in certain circumstances, reduce attractiveness or perceived attractiveness of green projects where they compete directly (e.g. natural gas vs. renewables; crude oil vs. biofuels and low-emission vehicles; crude oil when natural gas market is indexed)
2. Underlying project or activity-specific factors
2.1. Policy settings to adequately internalise environmental externalities
2.1.1. Low or non-existent price on carbon that lowers attractiveness of green projects *vis-à-vis* fossil fuels
2.1.2. Presence of fossil fuel subsidies which deteriorate economics of green projects
2.2. Policy ambition, certainty and stability
2.2.1. Policy support for projects or activities is non-existent, insufficient or not ambitious enough to incentivise investment
2.2.2. Policy support changed retroactively, reversed, cancelled or suddenly changed
2.2.3. Projects penalised (e.g. new taxes applied on renewable energy power generation)
2.2.4. Policy risk insurance options lacking
2.2.5. Policy support switched from support type that favours price stability (e.g. feed-in tariff) to support that creates revenue volatility (e.g. feed-in premium)

Note: 1. In rising-rate environments long-term refinancing through bond markets may be less attractive.

Table 2.A1.2 **Potential barriers specific to green bond market growth**

BARRIER
1. Lack of bankable pipeline of projects
1.1. A lack of preconditions and enabling environment for bond markets, investor base and green projects inhibit the emergence of bankable and investment-grade projects
1.2. Inherently small scale of certain green projects (e.g. distributed generation and energy efficiency) and lack of aggregation mechanisms restrict these projects from becoming "green bond-ready"
1.3. Absence of national infrastructure roadmaps and transparent, credible pipelines to communicate green bond opportunities
2. Instrument-related
2.1. Regulation
2.1.1. Lack of clear regulatory and legislative frameworks for specific bonds (e.g. lack of regulations for the offer, sale and trading of asset-backed securities, covered bonds, private placement, 144A[1])
2.2. Credit enhancement
2.2.1 Absence of a system for financial guarantees in some markets and monoline insurers to credit enhance bonds
2.3. Supporting market infrastructure and analytics
2.3.1. Lack of commonly accepted approach to distinguish among bonds in terms of their carbon intensity or their "greenness"
3. Supply side (issuer)
3.1. Regulation
3.1.1. Issuance regulation and procedures that are overly burdensome, leading to increased time and costs which change green bond attractiveness relative to other forms of debt
3.1.2. Absence of official sectoral regulation and guidance for certain types of green bonds (e.g. project bonds and public-private partnerships) restricts issuance
3.2. Knowledge and uncertainty
3.2.1. Dearth of knowledge among full range of issuers that bond issuance, let alone green bond issuance, may be an option
3.2.2. Definitional uncertainty for eligibility of certain green projects and activities for green bond issuance
3.2.3. Absence of official guidance on green bond issuance procedures and guidelines or uncertainty in how to apply voluntary guidelines
3.2.4. Confusion on the role and need for second- and third-party opinions, assurance and certifications
3.3. Transactions costs
3.3.1. Upfront and ongoing transaction costs from green labelling and associated administrative, certification, reporting, verification and monitoring requirements (cost estimates vary)
3.4. Additional factors: Risks
3.4.1. Reputational risk if a bond's green credentials are challenged
3.4.2. Investors may seek penalties for a "green default" whereby a bond is paid in full but issuer breaks agreed green clauses
4. Demand side (investor)
4.1. Regulation
4.1.1. Investment restrictions of a quantitative[2] and qualitative[3] nature that may duly or unduly limit allocations to bonds, including green bonds
4.1.2. Excessive government bond issuance and investor regulation that requires high domestic investor allocations to government bonds, crowding out non-government bonds, including green bonds
4.1.3. Lack of requirements to examine or disclose carbon intensity of portfolio
4.2. Knowledge
4.2.1. Limited experience among base of domestic institutional investors, lacking capacity to analyse and invest in green bonds
5. Definitions and standards
5.1. Lack of unified definitions and standards for green bonds, giving rise to confusion and the possibility for reputational risk if green integrity of bond questioned
5.2. Lack of co-operation between market players and across countries (e.g. different guidelines from different regulators)
5.3. Limited scope for legal enforcement of green integrity
5.4. Lack of standardisation that leads to complexities in investor research on green bonds and a need for extra due diligence that may not always be fulfilled

Notes: 1. In the United States, rule 144A is a safe harbour exemption from the registration requirements of Section 5 of the Securities Act for certain private offers and sales of qualifying securities to qualified institutional investors. It is credited with having increased the liquidity of the securities affected as they can be traded among qualified investors without certain registration requirements and transaction costs. 2. Quantitative restrictions could apply to proportions and values of assets held in different allocations. 3. Qualitative restrictions could apply to the nature and type of assets (e.g. non-government, corporate and asset-backed securities bonds), whether they are exchange listed, the credit rating level, etc.

Annex 2.A2.
Local currency bond markets and institutional investors

Local currency bond market

A local currency bond market (LCBM)[1] is the cornerstone of domestic financial markets and a necessary foundation for any domestic green bond market. The establishment of a local government bond market alongside issuance of bonds by supranationals targeting investments in a particular country can shape the structure of the corporate segment and lead the development of the fixed-income market more broadly, including subnational government debt and asset-backed securities (ABS) markets. Green bonds can be issued across all of these segments (although a sovereign green bond had yet to be issued as of October 2015).

A non-exhaustive list of preconditions to the development of LCBMs where green bonds can be issued include the need to develop: a domestic institutional investor base; a suitable issuance framework for a wholesale market; a credible credit rating framework; a long-term yield curve; a robust securitisation framework, including flexible special-purpose vehicles; a robust public-private partnership (PPP) framework; and a pipeline of bankable projects that can be financed or refinanced through bonds.

In response to the "G20 Action Plan to Support the Development of Local Currency Bond Markets (LCBMs)" (G20, 2011), the International Monetary Fund, the World Bank, the European Bank of Reconstruction and Development, and the OECD produced a diagnostic framework (IMF et al., 2013) that analyses the main elements necessary to deepen LCBMs in emerging and developing economies. The framework serves to analyse the state and efficiency of LCBMs and provides the basis for designing a strategy for market deepening with appropriate sequencing of policy action and delivery of associated technical assistance. As part of the G20's efforts to foster development of LCBMs, a range of international organisations[2] developed a shared database of advisory operations to help co-ordinate assistance across international institutions and update reports are issued for the G20 on an annual basis.

Policy makers can consult the diagnostic framework to address fundamental barriers to green bond market development and can take actions related to improving the macroeconomic policy framework, composition and needs of the issuer and investor base, primary and secondary market structures and related market dynamics, regulatory and legal frameworks, and market infrastructures.

Mobilising institutional investors

Once such preconditions are in place, the key to unlocking the potential of green bonds is to design financial structures that cater to the risk appetite of institutional investors. This is a challenge for both emerging and developing economies as well as for OECD countries. In this context, the availability of risk mitigation mechanisms, such as credit risk enhancements, can be helpful, especially for instruments such as project bonds, which generally struggle to receive an investment-grade rating on their own.

As reviewed by the OECD (Kaminker et al., 2013; Kaminker and Stewart, 2012), during the previous decade the provision of full guarantees on bond repayments by monoline insurers (see Glossary)[3] was successfully used in the United Kingdom and United States and in selected emerging economies, mainly Chile. However, most monolines stopped issuing financial guarantees in 2008 after their dramatic rating downgrades, including multiple bankruptcies. The challenge in the wake of the global financial crisis has been to develop new business models of risk sharing and credit enhancements, especially for project bonds. Initiatives in this area are at an early stage.

France and the United Kingdom have recently established programmes of government guarantees which operate in a manner similar to a monoline. The Overseas Private Investment Corporation (OPIC) – the US government's development finance institution – offers "green guaranties": US government guaranties[4] that adhere to the Green Bond Principles. The first-ever OPIC green guaranties were placed with eligible US investors in the domestic debt capital markets in September 2014 to support the construction of the Luz del Norte solar PV project in Chile – which will be, when completed, the largest photovoltaic project in Latin America.

At a regional level, the European Union-European Investment Bank Project Bond Initiative has a good chance of creating an effective substitute for the monoline model for infrastructure financing in Europe by providing up to 20% of first-loss credit protection for senior creditors via a funded or unfunded Project Bond Credit Enhancement mezzanine debt piece for both the construction and operation phases. The Asian Development Bank is currently developing a project bond credit enhancement product, based on the EU's experience. Larger emerging economies, such as Brazil and Mexico, have established schemes of partial credit guarantees via the domestic development banks. They have not yet been used to support issuance of project bonds (World Bank et al., 2014).

Notes

1. The term LCBMs encompasses government and corporate (financial and non-financial) domestic debt securities, which are defined as issues by residents in the local market in local currency, targeted to resident investors in the Bank for International Settlements securities statistics. Some foreign currency issues are included in these data, but they are small.

2. The World Bank Group in consultation with the staff of the International Monetary Fund, Asian Development Bank, African Development Bank, Inter-American Development Bank, European Bank for Reconstruction and Development, OECD, and the Bank for International Settlements.

3. One of the developments that facilitated the use of project bonds for infrastructure financing in the United States and other OECD countries was the establishment of an insurance market for bond repayments. In particular, the monoline insurance sector offered a product to investors whereby timely payment of interest and principal was guaranteed.

4. Guaranties, also known as government-guaranteed certificates of participation, are essentially project bonds with an OPIC (US government) guarantee – the investor is paid from project revenues, with an OPIC guarantee that they will be paid.

References

G20 (2011), "G20 Action Plan to Support the Development of Local Currency Bond Markets", www.g20.utoronto.ca/2011/2011-finance-action-plan-currency-111015-en.pdf.

IMF et al. (2013), "Local currency bond markets: A diagnostic framework", International Monetary Fund, Washington, DC, 9 July, www.oecd.org/daf/fin/public-debt/Local-Currency-Bond-Markets-Diagnostic-Framework-2013.pdf.

Kaminker, C. and F. Stewart (2012), "The role of institutional investors in financing clean energy", *OECD Working Papers on Finance, Insurance and Private Pensions*, No. 23, OECD Publishing, Paris, http://dx.doi.org/10.1787/5k9312v2116f-en.

Kaminker, C. et al. (2013), "Institutional investors and green infrastructure investments: Selected case studies", *OECD Working Papers on Finance, Insurance and Private Pensions*, No. 35, OECD Publishing, Paris, http://dx.doi.org/10.1787/5k3xr8k6jb0n-en.

World Bank et al. (2014), "2nd annual note on recent developments in local currency bond markets (LCBMs)", August.

Chapter 3.

A quantitative framework for analysing potential bond contributions in a low-carbon transition

This chapter proposes a framework for understanding possible directions of bond market evolution and for analysing the potential contribution that the bond markets can make to a low-carbon transition. It lays out scenarios providing the first quantifications of debt financing, and bond financing in particular, that would be required in order to meet a 2°C energy investment scenario. Starting with energy investment requirements at the national level estimated by the International Energy Agency for its 2°C scenarios (2DS), the analysis converts investments into their constituent equity and debt components. Focusing on debt, the analysis considers the role that the bond markets will need to play to finance this investment and connect bond supply with demand from institutional investors.

Organising framework

Objectives

This analysis contains the first quantifications of debt financing, and bond financing in particular, to meet the 2°C energy investment scenarios (2DS) set forth by the International Energy Agency (IEA).[1,2]

The objectives of this analysis are three-fold:

1. to assess how much debt finance is needed to meet the IEA's 2DS between 2015 and 2035 in the four markets studied
2. to assess how the bond market might evolve from 2015 to 2035 to provide part of these debt finance needs, taking into account projected policy and technology development as well as financial innovation
3. to analyse the implications of the transformation of the bond market for the institutional investors that have driven the growth of the green bond market to date.

Sectors assessed

The focus of this analysis is on bond financing for the renewable energy, energy efficiency and low-emission vehicle (LEVs)[3] sectors. According to the IEA (2014: 199), these sectors are key components of the low-carbon assets included in the 2DS (between 80-90% depending on the scenario as measured by total investment), and were selected because sufficiently granular data and assumptions for these sectors are available (to 2035). The scope extends only to the energy efficiency portion of building investment though investment in other forms of energy efficiency such as in industry is another integral component of the 2DS pathway. Other elements of aggregate green building investment are also likely to have significant potential for bond financing, but could not be included in the analysis.

Renewable energy, energy efficiency in building investment and LEVs accounted for 75%, or USD 50 billion out of USD 66 billion in outstanding labelled green bonds as of June 2015, and 79% of annual green labelled issuance in 2015. Other segments of labelled green bond and unlabelled climate bond markets relate to low-carbon public transportation, climate adaptation, clean water, waste management, agriculture and forestry and other key areas of environmentally-related investment (CBI/HSBC, 2015). These sectors are beyond the scope of this analysis (and some sectors like adaptation are not included in the IEA's 2DS figures) but are clearly important areas of green finance where the bond markets can (and do) play a significant role. As perspective, the CCICED (2015) estimates that in the People's Republic of China (hereafter "China") approximately 40% of "green investment" needs will be for low-carbon projects in the period 2014-20, with the other 60% being needed for sectors such as water (supply, savings and remediation), waste treatment, sewage, land remediation and industrial gas treatment.[4]

For simplicity, the analysis refers to bonds issued in the renewable energy, energy efficiency in buildings and LEV sectors as "low-carbon bonds", and does not speculate on what portion will be labelled green in 2035. In practice, as of 2015, 11% of the wider "climate-aligned" bond market was explicitly labelled as green and this share has been growing (CBI/HSBC, 2015). It is, however, difficult to predict what this share may be in 2035.[5]

Geographic coverage

The quantification in this analysis of the potential for future low-carbon bond financing covers China, the EU, Japan and the United States, which together represent 68% of the global annual energy sector supply investment needs (including fossil fuels) projected for the next 5 years, and 52% in 2035 in a 2DS (Table 3.1). These four markets were selected because they have significantly more established bond markets than other regions (along with sufficiently robust statistics that can be used for analysis). They are also the largest markets, accounting for 76%, or USD 74 trillion, of the global debt securities markets valued at USD 97 trillion in 2014. Debt securities outstanding from all sectors (government, corporate, municipal, ABS, etc.) amounted to USD 39 trillion in the United States, USD 21 trillion in the EU, USD 9.7 trillion in Japan and USD 4.3 trillion in China.[6] New (gross) debt securities issuances in 2014 amounted to USD 19 trillion in these markets.[7]

Table 3.1. **Annual investment needs for renewable energy, energy efficiency in buildings and low-emission vehicles in a 2DS compared to global energy sector needs, 2015-35**

2012 USD

	2015-20*	2021-25	2026-30	2031-35
Renewable energy, energy efficiency and low-emission vehicles investment needs in the four markets (China, EU, Japan and United States)	573 billion	1 315 billion	1 264 billion	2 262 billion
All global investment needs for energy supply and energy efficiency	839 billion	2 230 billion	2 404 billion	4 340 billion
Share	68%	59%	53%	52%

* Figures are annualised over the five-year periods.

Source: OECD analysis based on IEA (2014), *World Energy Investment Outlook*, www.iea.org/publications/freepublications/publication/WEIO2014.pdf; IEA (2012), *Energy Technology Perspectives 2012: Pathways to a Clean Energy System*, http://dx.doi.org/10.1787/energy_tech-2012-en.

Methodology

In its *World Energy Investment Outlook* (2014) and *Energy Technology Perspectives* (2012), the IEA estimated investment needs in the renewable energy, energy efficiency and LEV sectors to 2035, based on scenarios in which countries take policy actions leading to a 2°C emissions pathway. Building on these investment scenarios, this analysis applies assumptions based on current trends in regional financial markets to synthetically breakdown the aggregated investment needs by source of finance and type of financial instrument (see Annex 3.A1 for methodology and assumptions). Figure 3.1 shows the steps of the decomposition and the main issues addressed in each step.

The input data for the scenarios discussed in this report relate to investment needs and capital structure (i.e. the shares of debt and equity needed, by sector and country). The investment data and decomposition by sector were provided by the IEA. A matching set of global assumptions were made (e.g. the split between utility scale and rooftop solar PV) and were referenced from a wide variety of public sources. These assumptions are set forth in Annex 3.A1. The estimates presented here are a function of the assumptions made, and are subject to significant uncertainty around policy, current commercial and financial practice, and future changes in these practices (Box 3.1). By setting forth these assumptions in a transparent manner, the analysis allows for close scrutiny and hopefully improved calibration of the model as updated assumptions become available.

Figure 3.1. **Flow diagram showing steps taken in developing a quantitative model and analytical framework**

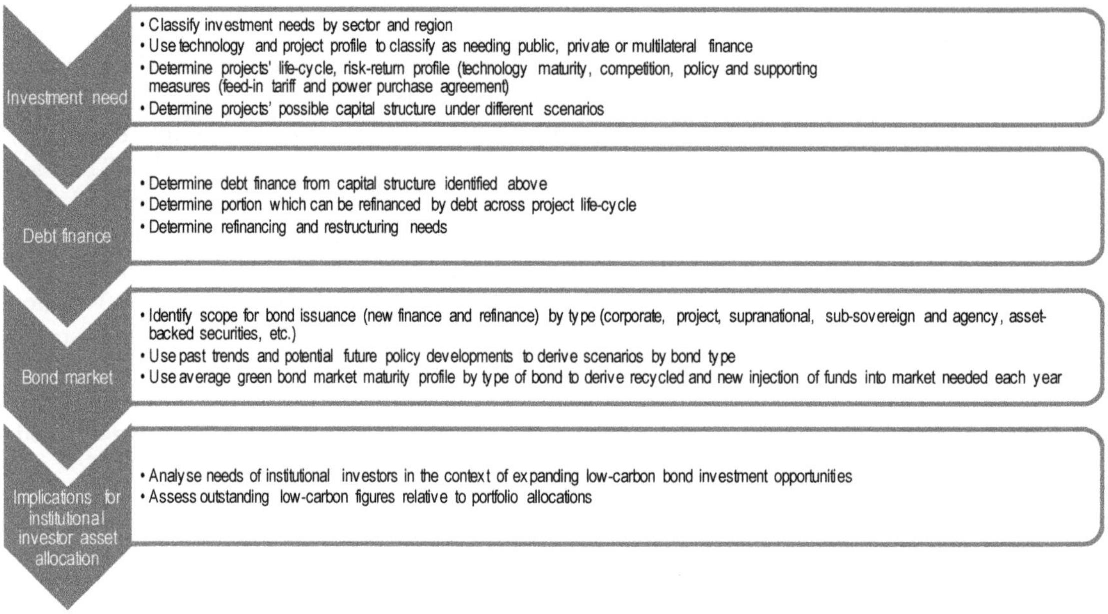

Box 3.1. Methodology

As detailed in Annex 3.A1, models were constructed for the four geographic markets and assumption-based scenarios were run to generate the output data. Input data and assumptions for the scenarios relate to investment need and capital structure. Data from current trends in regional financial markets are used to establish benchmark levels of leverage (measured as debt-to-equity ratios) and proportions of bond finance, by type and for each investment class. The investment data and decomposition by sector are all provided by the Innternational Energy Agency.

When a level of disaggregation proved insufficient, it was supplemented through a set of global assumptions, e.g. the split between utility scale and rooftop photovoltaics (PV), drawn from a range of sources (see Annex 3.A1 and references). Where data were unavailable, assumptions were constructed to simulate values and a sensitivity analysis was performed to determine the impact of these assumptions on key model outputs, then validated through consultation with market and industry experts.

There are three principal areas of uncertainty in these scenario estimates. First, uncertainty lies in the strength and mix of support policy that will be adopted and the evolution of technology and performance costs.

Second, uncertainty exists in current data on financial structures and sources of finance. Some markets are better documented than others. Securities regulations generally require that public market transactions be thoroughly and publicly documented – and therefore easier to analyse. However, a substantial portion of financial market transactions are private or unlisted and have limited disclosure of deal specifics. In these cases, third-party market analysis is the only option, rather than primary audited financial reports.

Third, financial practices may change. Although traditional financing structures may well continue, waves of financial innovation are often driven by changes in regulation, market preferences, corporate balance sheets, tax structures, financial crises and other factors. The types of financial structures deployed may be profoundly affected by such market shifts. For instance, China's debt markets have been characterised by banks providing significant lending to state-owned enterprises. These markets have experienced challenges and the financial system is undergoing significant change. As such, there are significant uncertainties regarding the future role of bond financing for low-carbon infrastructure. At the same time, the government has prioritised the development of green bond markets (PBoC/UNEP, 2015).

The scenarios in this report are based on the results of quantitative modelling. The modelling translates existing investment projections into types of financial structure, segmenting the results into selected regional and sectoral markets, and takes into account the suitability of financial structures for assets of different risk profiles over the asset's life, from development and construction through to operation (Figure 3.2). It is assumed that market actors will seek to optimise the capital structure and asset financing methods (and thereby minimise the cost of capital for their investments) wherever possible in line with prevailing and expected market circumstances and other economic variables that influence such decisions.

Figure 3.2. **The phases of asset development at individual and market level**

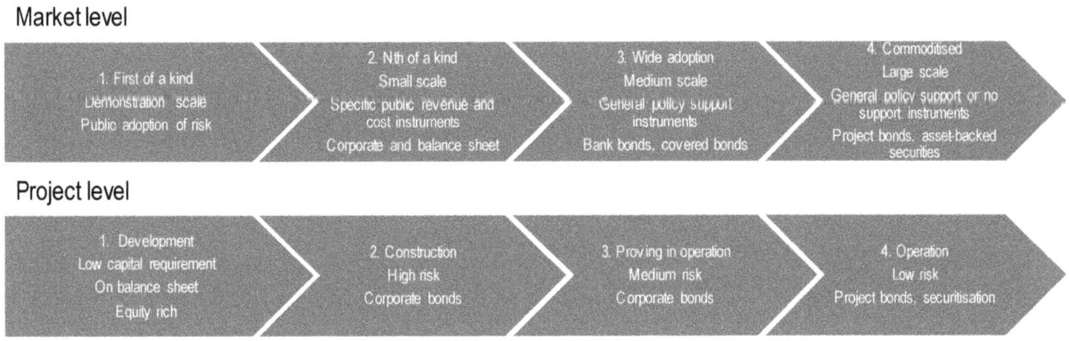

Two main scenarios were modelled and are presented in this analysis and in the annexes to this chapter, with both assuming that the world is on a 2DS pathway: 1) a base case scenario that uses conservative asset securitisation assumptions (projecting levels observed in the market in 2015 forwards); and 2) a scenario with a 10% increase in asset securitisation rate across all sectors (which represents a still conservative growth assumption that could be achieved through basic policy and market enablers targeted at securitisation). Both main scenarios assume policy makers adopt supportive policies to overcome challenges as described by OECD et al. (2016).

Figure 3.3 illustrates a further range of possible scenarios not described in the report. The top solid line illustrating the market growth potential represents the enhanced securitisation scenario 2, and represents a theoretical upper limit for the base case of low-carbon bonds outstanding in the sectors modelled if the world is on a 2DS, given capital structures and investment needs. The other lower lines illustrate, over a ten-year period, the speed at which the theoretical potential might be reached, depending on how the bond market develops. If there is a concerted push in China, the European Union, Japan and the United States to develop a low-carbon bond market, the growth rate over the first five years could be in the region of 100-200%. The historical growth of other bond markets suggests that there is a catalytic element embedded in market growth, whereby successively deeper and more liquid markets serve to further accelerate growth.

On the other hand, if the policy and regulatory environment is not conducive to rapid market growth, actual low-carbon bond issuance will fall behind its potential and may never reach it, as growth path 1 illustrates. If governments do not set policies to drive a transition to a low-carbon economy or 2DS, bond financing, as a function of the level of low-carbon infrastructure deployment, would be even lower still. While policies enabling the use of bonds to finance renewable energy, energy efficiency in buildings and LEVs are important, they do not drive demand for investment. Fundamental drivers of investment include targets and support measures, carbon pricing, inefficient fossil fuel subsidy removal and reform, research, development and demonstration policies, and other actions to facilitate investment in low-carbon infrastructure. Debt will necessarily play an important role in the financing of this infrastructure investment, and bonds could potentially make up an important portion of this debt. Ultimately, however, credible and consistent energy and climate policy and the economics of the sectors will be the drivers of investment over the next 20 years.

Figure 3.3. **Illustration of scenarios for how the low-carbon bond market could evolve**

USD billion

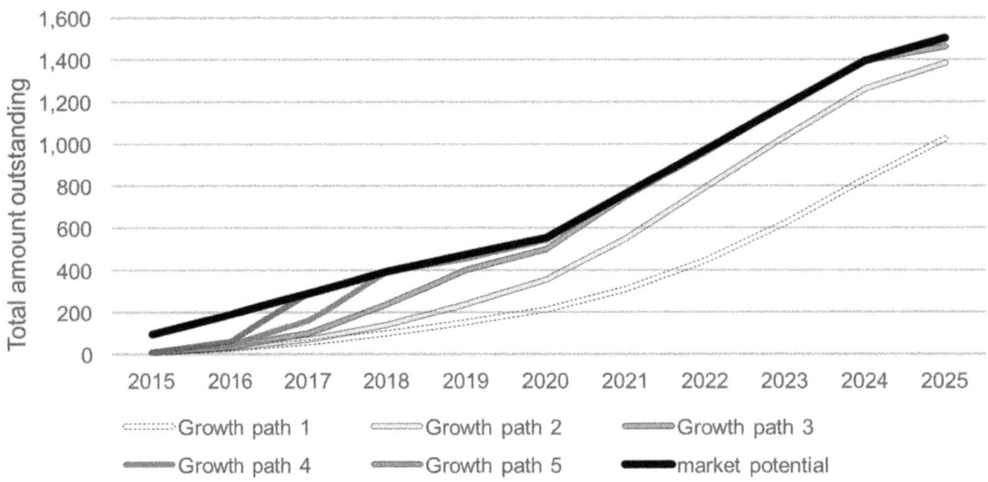

Note: The graph ends at 2025 to highlight possible evolutionary pathways in earlier years. Growth paths 1-5 are illustrative.

High-level quantitative results

Debt-to-equity breakdown

Figure 3.4 shows how total investment needs are financed in the baseline scenario, which takes current financing practices for the sectors studies and projects them forward. Debt (lending) is seen as covering 60% of total investment needs between 2015 and 2025, while this ratio decreases to 56% in 2030 and 52% in 2035. The mix of financing types ranges significantly across the types of assets, and changes over time. It is driven by increasing sectoral investment needs as technologies mature, for renewable energy but more significantly for LEVs which represent a disproportionately large share of future investment needs post-2025, according to the IEA (2015).[8]

Current trends in financing asset and durable consumption purchases show that a significant proportion of energy efficiency, distributed solar PV and LEV investment is done through consumer finance (i.e. loans provided to consumers by commercial banks and leases) or equity (i.e. “self-finance”, such as an LEV purchased in cash without any financing). Assuming that this continues to be the case, and given the large size of LEV and energy efficiency investment needs relative to renewables, equity and self-finance are estimated to continue to make a large contribution to financing low-carbon energy investment. Given the predominant role of equity and self-finance for LEVs, they take on a much larger share of all financing as LEV investments take on a larger share of total investments.

Figure 3.4. **Synthetic investment breakdown for the IEA 2DS by type of finance needed to 2035**

Annual basis, USD 2012

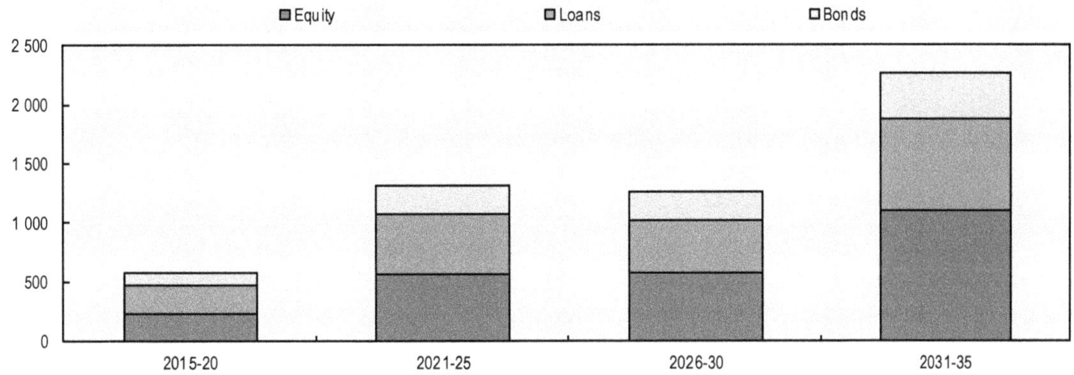

Note: Financial sector bonds that raise proceeds for on-lending not shown but represented in loan figures.

Source: OECD analysis based on IEA (2014), *World Energy Investment Outlook*, www.iea.org/publications/freepublications/publication/WEIO2014.pdf; IEA (2012), *Energy Technology Perspectives 2012: Pathways to a Clean Energy System*, http://dx.doi.org/10.1787/energy_tech-2012-en.

The role of bonds in financing investment depends on the maturity of the technology, the characteristics of the projects – including the scale at project level, as well as the type of investor. The scenarios break down the IEA's aggregate investment figures by type of asset (Figure 3.5). The use of debt to finance LEV and energy efficiency is around 50%, with a much higher proportion (around 75%) seen in the renewable energy sector. Bonds, as a form of debt capital, will therefore be able to play a more prominent role proportion-wise for renewable energy than for low-emission vehicles and energy efficiency. However, due to the sheer scale of financing needed, the USD figure for debt (and bonds) issued to finance LEV and energy efficiency is seen as significantly higher.

Figure 3.5. **The mix of equity, loans and bonds varies across sector and by timeframe**

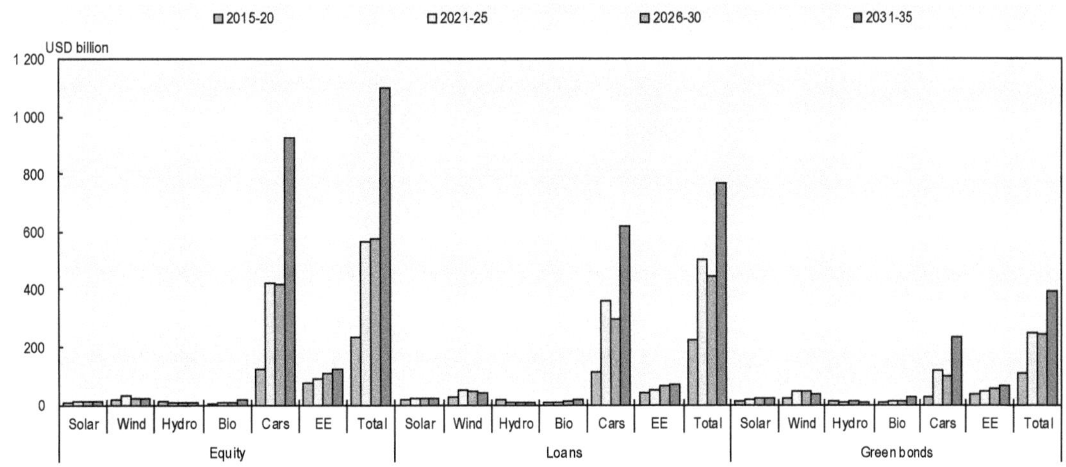

Notes: EE: energy efficiency. Financial sector bonds that raise proceeds for on-lending are not shown but represented in loan figures.

A large proportion of the investment needs in energy efficiency is estimated by the IEA to be needed for lighting and appliances. The IEA estimates that up to 60% of global investment needs in transport, buildings and industry-related energy efficiency will be self-financed (with cash). LEVs will also be financed largely by internal sources of finance, especially in China where car purchases by households and businesses do not materially rely on external finance.[9] Only 30% of the investment needs in LEVs by households in China are estimated to be financed through capital markets.

High-level results in context

After having examined the aggregate debt, bond and equity proportions implied by the investment needs, the work then considers the types of debt instruments and bonds that would be suitable for each type of asset. The results of the analysis suggest that by 2035 in a 2DS, bonds financing and refinancing the three sectors in the four markets studied have the potential to scale to as much as USD 4.7-5.6 trillion in outstanding securities globally and USD 620-720 billion in annual issuance with the ranges representing a base-case "low securitisation" scenario and an "enhanced securitisation" scenario, respectively (Figure 3.6).[10] While these figures may seem large on an absolute basis, they are small (approximately 4%) relative to the scale of issuance in debt securities markets generally, with USD 19 trillion of gross issuance in China, the EU, Japan and the United States in 2014.[11]

Figure 3.6. **Scenario results to 2035 compared with low-carbon investment needs and new debt securities issuance**

Annual

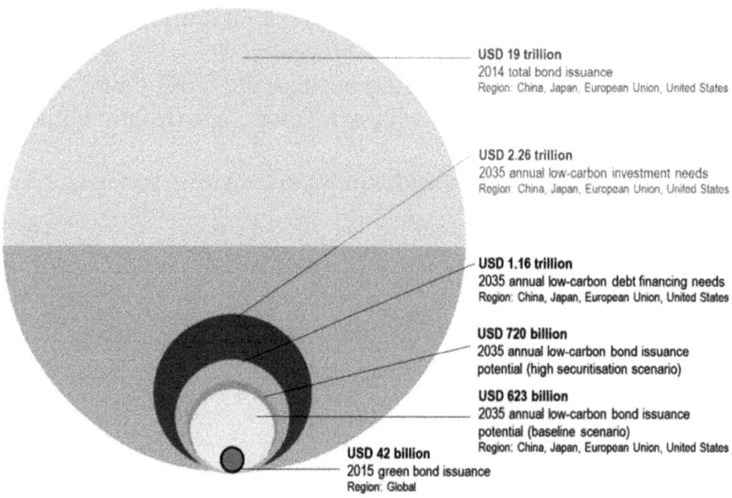

Note: OECD modelling scenarios and annual "low-carbon" investment needs in the figure cover the renewable energy, energy efficiency and low-emissions vehicle sectors as estimated by the IEA (2014, 2012). The 2015 green bond issuance figure of USD 42 billion is provided as a reference point and extends to all sectors included in *Climate Bonds Initiative database*. No judgement is made as to the percentage of bonds from these "low-carbon" sectors that will be labelled as "green bonds". Annual total bond issuance is provided as an illustration and just as with green bond issuance, reflects "gross issuance" figures, i.e. does not account for those securities that reach maturity or are redeemed from previous years (termed "net issuance"). It includes other types of debt securities such as notes and money market instruments.

Source: OECD analysis based on IEA (2014), *World Energy Investment Outlook*, www.iea.org/publications/freepublications/publication/WEIO2014.pdf; IEA (2012), *Energy Technology Perspectives 2012: Pathways to a Clean Energy System*, http://dx.doi.org/10.1787/energy_tech-2012-en; Climate Bonds Initiative, BIS, SIFMA, ECB, JSRI, ADB and Goldman Sachs data.

The analysis suggests that the 2020s have the potential to be the start of the "golden years" for bond issuance in the low-carbon sectors. As low-carbon technologies mature, they become more familiar to bond markets, which will be substantial contributors to the financing and refinancing of new-build assets. The two main scenarios presented in Figure 3.6 represent the aforementioned baseline scenario and an "enhanced securitisation" scenario with a 10% increase in ABS-type bonds issued indicated by error bars in Figure 3.7, which shows issuance and outstanding bonds. The latter scenario is useful to consider because it could occur if certain policies targeted at enhancing securitisation markets (as discussed in Chapter 2) are adopted beyond those in the core scenario.

Figure 3.7. **Potential for low-carbon bond issuance ranges between USD 620 billion and USD 720 billion per year by 2035**

USD billion

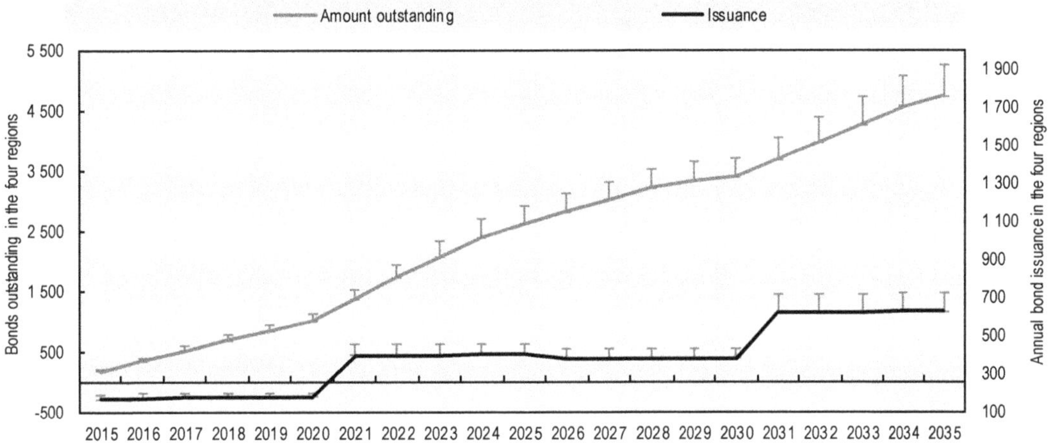

Note: Error bars represent the enhanced securitisation scenario, based on a 10% increase in asset securitisation rate across all sectors over the baseline scenario, which incorporates a more conservative asset securitisation assumption. "Outstanding" refers to cumulative amount of bonds issued that have not yet reached redemption or maturity.

As the risks of assets fall, as policy stabilises and as the capital markets become more familiar with the low-carbon sector, the role played by bonds could expand rapidly as demonstrated by historical precedent throughout the traditional energy and infrastructure sectors (Dewar, 2011).[12] Figure 3.8 exhibits the potential for different types of bonds to finance a range of sectors and sub-sectors of low-carbon investments studied. It displays a picture of the volume of outstanding securities through to 2035 and the speed at which they could potentially scale up.

Results by type of bond[13]

Financial sector bonds

The results shown in Figures 3.4 and 3.5 reveal the prominent role loans can play in financing low-carbon investment needs to 2035. Financial institutions (including banks and non-bank intermediaries) are expected to continue to be the largest provider of loans to all three sectors given their specific expertise in the arranging of credit for the earlier stages of infrastructure development project cycle, from planning to construction through to project operation, when other sources of debt capital – including bond markets – can be called on to refinance the debt. While financial institutions have a major role to play in arranging the debt financing for low-carbon infrastructure through loans and through underwriting and investing in bonds, they notably also can act as issuers of "financial sector" bonds as is shown in Figures 3.9-3.12.

Figure 3.8. **Potential and speed of scale-up for bonds outstanding varies by type of bond, sector and sub-sector**

Baseline scenario

Sector	Year	Value in 2035 (USD billion)	Bonds outstanding by sector and type
Photovoltaic	Municipal/sov.	62	
	SSA	20	
	Corporate	69	
	Project bond	46	
	Asset-backed securities	104	
Wind	Municipal/sov.	46	
	SSA	66	
	Corporate	236	
	Project bond	116	
	Asset-backed securities	157	
Energy efficiency	Municipal/sov.	268	
	SSA	115	
	Corporate	200	
	Project bond	0	
	Asset-backed securities	1 101	
Bioenergy	Municipal/sov.	5	
	SSA	15	
	Corporate	50	
	Project bond	47	
	Asset-backed securities	29	
Hydro energy	Municipal/sov.	9	
	SSA	26	
	Corporate	88	
	Project bond	61	
	Asset-backed securities	55	
Total	Municipal/sov.	390	
	SSA	241	
	Corporate	643	
	Project bonds	270	
	Asset-backed securities and CLO	1 447	
	Financial sector	1 741	
	Total	4 732	

Notes: CLO: collaterised loan obligation. "Outstanding" refers to cumulative amount of bonds issued that have not yet reached redemption or maturity. Shades of grey do not represent uniform values and are illustrations of magnitude of outstanding bonds as a share of the 2035 total for a particular sector and type of bond.

Financial institutions rely to a large extent on bonds to raise capital for their lending activities, with US and EU commercial banks currently maintaining a bond-to-loan ratio of 30% (Bielenberg et al., 2016; ECB, 2015). Commercial banks are among the most active and prominent users of bonds markets to raise capital for their lending activities. In the United States and the EU, 42% and 48% respectively of outstanding debt securities had been issued by financial institutions in 2014 (ECB, 2015).

Financial institutions are expected to continue to use bond markets to raise capital to finance their low-carbon related lending, which can lead to financial sector issuance of bonds that finance this on-balance sheet lending (referred to as "on-lending"). An example of this type of bond in the market today is ABN AMRO's EUR 500 green bond issued in 2015 where the proceeds are used to finance and refinance "green loans" that finance solar panels installed on residential buildings as well as commercial real estate loans for the construction and financing of energy efficiency buildings.

Unlike ABS and collateralised loan obligations (CLOs), bonds issued by bank treasuries will not be directly backed by green assets. However, as is seen in the case of "use of proceeds"[14] corporate bonds, a link can be established between the capital raised by a bond and how it is put to use in financing low-carbon investment. Figure 3.9 shows a scenario for bond issuance by the financial sector, keeping assumptions based on the market today constant and the corresponding amount in outstanding bonds issued by financial institutions between 2015 and 2035. This segment of the market has the potential to add up to USD 1 trillion to total bonds outstanding in 2025 and USD 1.7 trillion in 2035 (out of a market of USD 4-5 trillion).

Figure 3.9. **Bonds issued by the financial sector exhibit significant potential to scale**

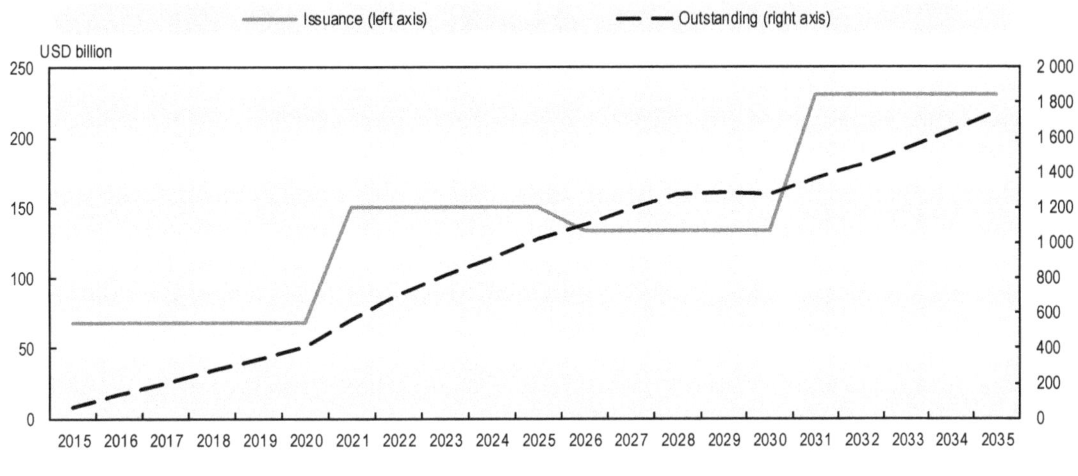

Note: Financial sector issuance of bonds assumes a bond-to-loan ratio of 30% in all modelled markets.

Figure 3.10 presents a complete view of how almost USD 2.3 trillion of annual low-carbon investment needs in the sectors and markets studied in the period 2031-35 could be financed. In order to distinguish between bonds which directly finance and refinance investment needs (i.e. projects) from financial sector bonds which fund bank loans for projects, the figures for financial sector issuance are presented separately from other bonds and as a derivative of loans.

Asset-backed securities

Revitalising the concept of securitisation, which was tarnished during the 2008-10 financial crisis, is important to the scaling up of low-carbon infrastructure finance and has emerged as a key area of focus for policy makers (Segoviano et al., 2015). A healthy market for securitisation can deliver significant financial benefits.[15] Efforts by policy makers geared at mitigating risks and ensuring that securitisation markets contribute to economic growth and financial stability include the EU's Capital Markets Union Action Plan,[16] the Solar Access to Public Capital Initiative[17] in the United States and initiatives elsewhere, including in China (EC, 2016; CBI/LSE, 2015; US DOE/NREL, 2015; Segoviano et al., 2015). This revitalisation can be achieved in large measure by standardising the assets and by making the securitisation process, and the market activity it spurs, safer, simpler and more transparent. Any efforts to support green securitisation must be undertaken in a prudent, judicious and transparent manner so that ABS markets emerge with integrity and with due consideration for any financial stability issues.

Figure 3.10. **Financing in 2035 by type of capital and bond (baseline scenario)**

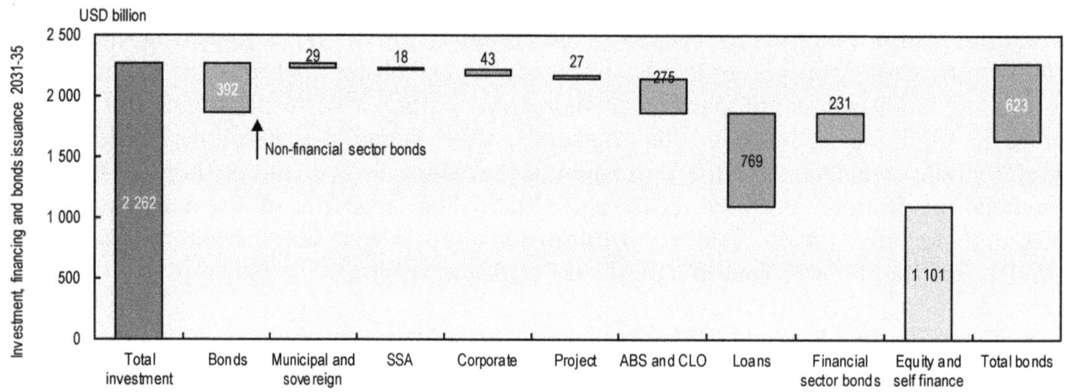

Notes: SSA: supranational, sub-sovereign and agency; ABS: asset-backed securities; CLO: collateralised loan obligation. Bonds are coloured in grey and financial sector bonds appear after loans to reflect issuance that finances on-lending via banks.

There is potential for a significant expansion in the origination and subsequent issuance of ABS as perceived risks fall. Standardisation of projects and policy support can enable the pooling of individual loans, which effectively ties bonds to a group of assets, rather than individual assets. Compared to project bonds that generally back individual projects (or collections of larger scale assets concentrated in wind and solar "farms"), ABS are more efficient vehicles for aggregating pools of individual loans.

ABS have a disproportionately large potential since they are less likely to be constrained by government fiscal and budgetary constraints in the case of government (i.e. municipal) bonds, and by balance sheet constraints[18] in the case of corporate and SSA bonds seen as accounting for USD 240 billion and 640 billion (8% and 14%) of bonds outstanding in 2035. Annual ABS and CLO issuance is seen as having the potential to reach USD 280-380 billion in the 2031-35 period in the baseline and enhanced securitisation scenarios, respectively (or between 44% and 52% of annual issuance).

The prominent role that could be played by securitisation and issuance of ABS and CLOs rests on two arguments. First, as new technologies mature and track records develop, the perceived risks of ABS and CLOs and need to assess risk on a project-by-project basis will decrease. Standardisation of technologies and contracts will allow for pooling of loans and leases, and for bonds to be backed by a group of assets, rather than individual assets. Second, there is a need to move away from the constraints of balance sheet financing in order to scale up investments to the quantum needed in a 2DS. If market forces and policy makers come together to facilitate and rejuvenate the securitisation process in a judicious and transparent way (see Chapter 2), a pipeline of financially attractive projects (due to a mix of policies, policy support, standardisation and technology cost reductions) will emerge that can benefit from increased financing flows beyond the limits imposed by balance sheet constraints of a structural and regulatory nature on power companies and banks.

Figure 3.11. **Asset-backed and financial sector bonds have the largest potential to scale up (baseline scenario)**

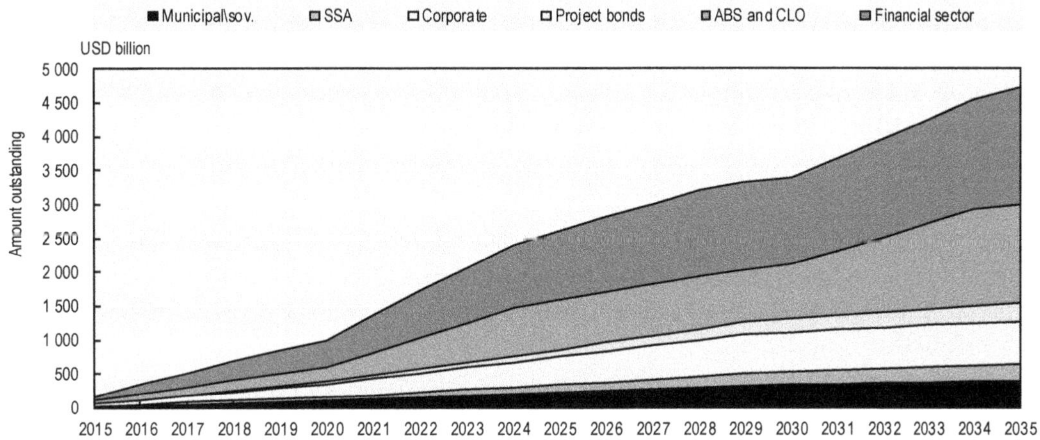

Notes: SSA: supranational, sub-sovereign and agency; ABS = asset-backed security; CLO = collateralised loan obligation. The figure depicts the base case "low-securitisation scenario". Bonds in the People's Republic of China, Japan, the EU and the United States.

LEVs, distributed and small-scale power generation have significant potential for asset securitisation. Projects within each of these categories share financial characteristics and can be standardised and homogenised, allowing for pooling of projects. The automotive market is seen as having the greatest opportunity, driven by current trends in car loan and lease securitisation combined with large replacement investment needs in transport to 2035, except in China where there is an increase in vehicle ownership. Hence, the analysis indicates that ABS increases in market share over time as the ABS market develops in China. Securitisation of LEV leases are seen as a particularly suitable target, as demonstrated by ABS issued in 2014 and 2015 from Toyota. Accordingly, by 2035 in the baseline scenario, almost a third of outstanding bonds from the low-carbon sectors studied could be in the form of ABS.

Securitised energy efficiency loans have the potential to make up 18% of ABS outstanding in 2025 and 13% in 2035. These are likely to constitute a minor part of the potential that green mortgages are thought to have to finance the full value of efficient buildings. Green mortgages could eventually be securitised into green collateralised mortgage obligations.

Project bonds

Project bonds are also likely to grow in line with the general expansion in low-carbon physical asset deployment, enhanced through specific policy support measures such as credit enhancement. Annual issuance is seen as having the potential to reach around USD 30 billion in the 2031-35 period (accounting for 4% of all low-carbon bond issuance). While ABS are a more efficient investment vehicle for aggregating smaller projects and loans, project bonds can support large-scale assets such as off-shore wind, geothermal, hydro and enabling infrastructure such as interconnectors, as well as larger wind and solar farms. As of 2016, all of these sectors had featured project bond financing.[19]

Sovereign, sub-sovereign, municipal and agency bonds

The share of municipal, sub-sovereign and sovereign bonds could grow over time but is seen as constrained by public finance limits and the fiscal capacities of governments. Annual issuance is seen as having the potential to reach around USD 50 billion in the 2031-35 period (accounting for 8% of all low-carbon bond issuance). Public financial institutions such as development banks and agencies could theoretically increase their issuance if their capitalisation is increased, but this prospect is not modelled due to uncertainty. Efforts to expand the creditworthiness and ability of cities to issue bonds could positively impact these figures in emerging and developing economies.

The main use of public borrowing is seen as financing municipal programmes to improve the energy efficiency of buildings and support renewable energy deployment. A sovereign green bond was issued for the first time in December 2016 as mentioned in Chapter 1. Figure 3.12 illustrates the growth and share of various types of bonds between 2015 and 2035.

Further details are revealed in the waterfall charts shown in Figure 3.12. The share of bond issuance in total investment starts at 31% in 2015 and falls slightly to 28% in 2035 due to a higher share of vehicle finance. The share of equity rises from 41% in 2015 to 49% in 2035 while loans fall steadily from 39% to 34%. Corporate bonds, including those issued by financial institutions, have the potential to account for the largest share of bond issuance in the 2015-20 period, with 56%, while ABS and CLOs[20] may account for 23%. However the amount of ABS and CLO issuance has the potential to rise significantly to 44-46% of total issuance in 2035, whereas corporate issuance falls to 44% and 41% in the baseline scenario and enhanced securitisation scenarios, respectively. SSA and government bonds, are seen as falling from 14% to 8% over the period.

Corporate bonds are seen as continuing to play an important role, raising financing for a variety of assets. Corporate bonds could dominate the universe of bonds outstanding with a 60% share during the early stage of market development. This share is also seen as falling to 50% in 2035 while ABS and CLO shares may increase from 20% at the start of the period to 30% in 2035. These trends illustrate a trend of early market development led by corporate issuance. However, as markets mature, the size of ABS and CLO markets will take a more prominent role, as is the case with many other debt securities markets. The reason for this change is embedded in both the higher securitisation rate in the later stages of market development and the greater prominence LEV investment will need to take toward the later stages of the period. Policy makers will need to play an important role to permit and facilitate this transition. They can do so by creating a regulatory environment that minimises risks (i.e. by ensuring that securitisations are done prudently and provide sufficient transparency), while helping to kick-start the market through certain methods (as discussed in Chapter 2).

Geographic results and variations

Results obtained for individual markets highlight geographical variations and some similarities. For instance, financial sector issuance potential is seen as strong in all four of the markets, and the financial sector accounts for the largest low-carbon bond sector in China, the EU and Japan (Figure 3.13). The following section describes the potential for

Figure 3.12. **Annual investment breakdown by source of finance and bonds outstanding in all four regions**

Baseline scenario

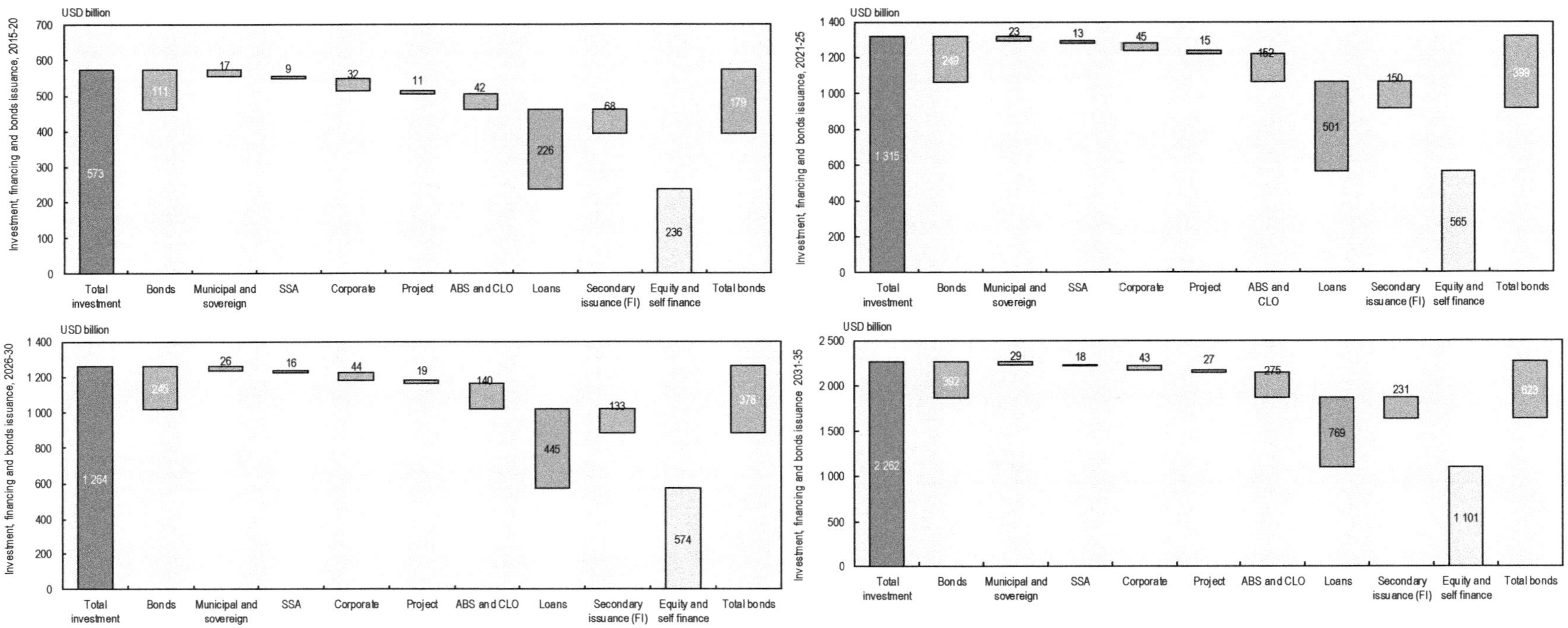

Notes: SSA: supranational, sub-sovereign and agency; ABS = asset-backed security; CLO = collateralised loan obligation.

Figure 3.13. **Regional variations are significant across the four markets studied by 2035**

A. Total bonds outstanding in 2035 in the United States

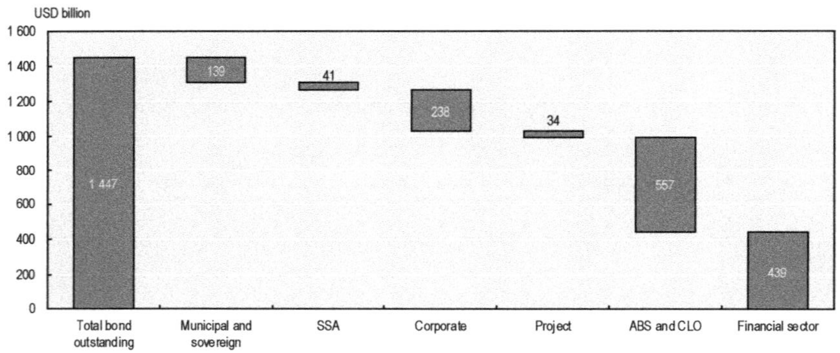

B. Total bonds outstanding in 2035 in the People's Republic of China

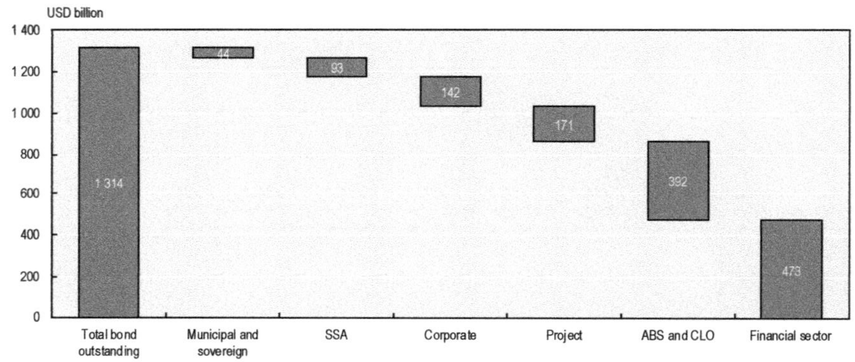

C. Total bonds outstanding in 2035 in Japan

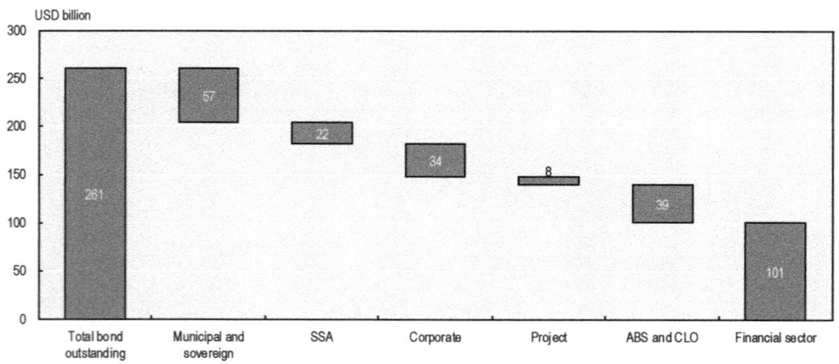

D. Total bonds outstanding in 2035 in the European Union

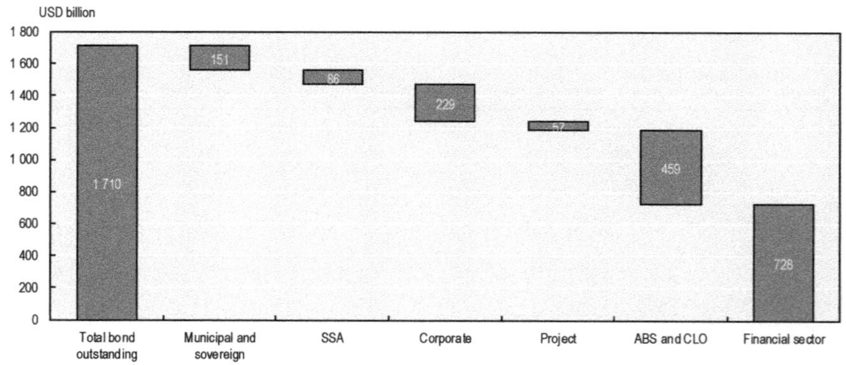

Notes: SSA: supranational, sub-sovereign and agency; ABS = asset-backed security; CLO = collateralised loan obligation. Annex 3.A3 can be referred to for detailed modelling results for each market.

the market in 2035 in terms of outstanding bonds, and provides geographic overviews along with snapshots of the annual issuance potential by 2020. Complete results by geography, asset and financing type are given in Annex 3.A3.

United States

In the United States, a higher share of ABS is seen as possible than in the other markets in 2035 (which have much lower shares of ABS currently), with ABS representing the largest share followed closely by financial sector bonds. This is due to the higher level of maturity of the financial markets in general and securitisation rates and markets in particular in the United States. The US mortgage-backed securities (MBS) market currently represents 60% of all mortgage debt outstanding in the United States[21] and the US auto loan ABS market is also relatively mature with a 20% securitisation rate of total vehicle expenditure (SIFMA, 2015).[22] In practice, some challenges could impede the growth of asset securitisation, for example in the solar industry. However, at least some of these barriers can be overcome through financial structuring (Lowder and Mendelsohn, 2013).

US utilities are among the highest users of bond finance, and are reflected as such in this analysis. Over time it is assumed that a portion of corporate borrowing by US utilities will be substituted by project bonds and ABS. The analysis suggests US utilities could be a more important contributor to corporate bond issuances than in other regions, accounting for 30% of US corporate bond issuance in 2025, declining to 25% in 2035. US utilities are very active in the efficient US corporate bond market today, but a question remains as to what extent corporate balance sheets (assuming the same universe of companies, without capital from new entrants) can sustain the incremental levels of investment required by a 2DS scenario. If balance sheets become strained by the amount of investment needed, substitution of corporate issuance with project bonds and ABS may become an attractive alternative.

US municipal authorities issue bonds to finance their infrastructure-related expenditure and are expected to continue to do so. Similarly, SSA and development banks are seen as having a role to play with state-sponsored "green investment banks" in Connecticut and Hawaii already active in mobilising the debt capital markets for low-carbon investment (OECD, 2016a). Budget constraints, however, are expected to prevent municipalities and SSA bond issuers from scaling up their issuances to match the pace of corporate issuers, and ABS securitisations. Municipal, sub-sovereign and sovereign and SSA issuances could account for 3% of total outstanding by 2035.

European Union

Similar to the United States, the EU features significant potential for ABS issuance, but the financial sector is seen as playing a more prominent role than in the United States. ABS is seen as accumulating a large market share but cedes some of this share over time to corporate and project bonds. The increase in project bonds reflects assumptions that include policy support such as the Project Bond Credit Enhancement Initiative undertaken by the European Investment Bank and the European Commission, which is targeted at increasing reliance on bond financing at the project level.

Corporate bond issuance has the potential to be very significant given the active role European utilities have played in the EU corporate bond market. Governments could be strongly involved in raising funds through the bond market to implement energy efficiency and renewable energy programmes. Many options are possible in Europe and much will depend on the direction policy takes and the strength of corporate utility balance sheets, which have deteriorated in recent years.

Figure 3.14. **Annual investment, financing and bond issuance potential in the United States by 2020**

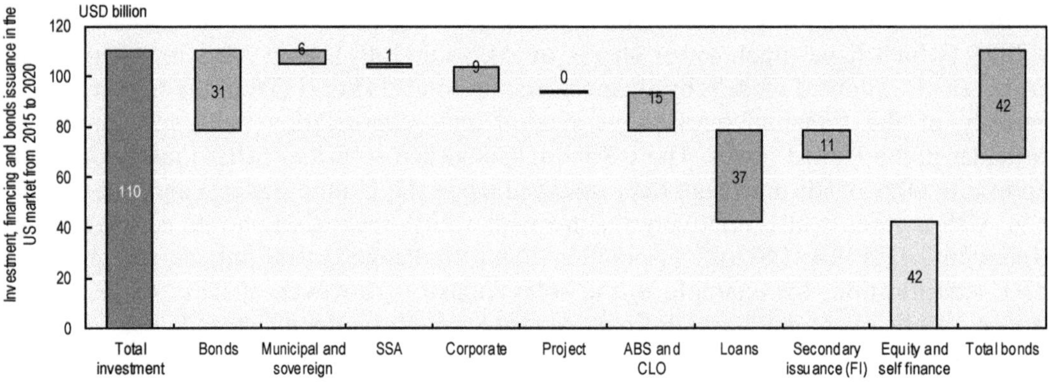

Notes: SSA: supranational, sub-sovereign and agency; ABS = asset-backed security; CLO = collateralised loan obligation.

Figure 3.15. **Annual investment, financing and bond issuance potential in the European Union by 2020**

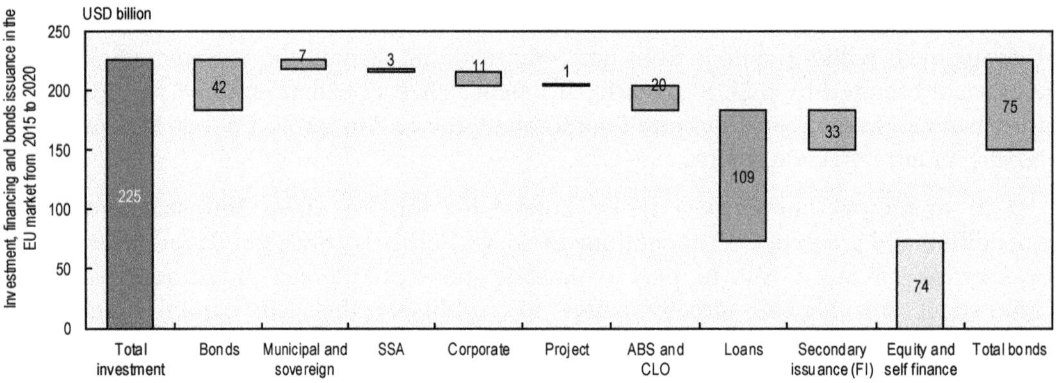

Notes: SSA: supranational, sub-sovereign and agency; ABS = asset-backed security; CLO = collateralised loan obligation.

China[23]

In China, corporate and project bonds could take the greater share while ABS could expand gradually alongside a maturing debt capital market. In 2025, half of the low-carbon bonds outstanding could be issued by corporates, particularly the financial sector. Currently Chinese non-financial corporates are predominantly reliant on bank lending. Only 6% of all debt outstanding in 2013 was in the form of debt securities, though this is projected to increase to 15% between 2014 and 2018 (Standard & Poor's Ratings Services, 2014). China's state-owned enterprises and the "quasi-public" sector including banks have been largely successful in issuing infrastructure bonds and creating a market for these bonds. Between 2009 and 2013, an estimated 80% of infrastructure debt was raised through infrastructure bonds. The prospect of participation by financial and corporate entities in China was realised in early 2016 following the release of guidance, regulations and requirements for green bond issuance by the People's Bank of China (PBoC).

The high proportion of bond finance for infrastructure projects and low reliance on bond finance by Chinese corporates is reflected in this analysis, which assumes an average bond proportion of 47% in the capital structure of renewables project finance and a 20% bond share in corporate finance by power utilities. Project bonds in China currently enjoy a boost to their credit rating since they are usually assumed to benefit from a guarantee from the state (Ehlers, Packer and Remolona, 2014; Ehlers, 2014).

Asset securitisation has only been introduced relatively recently in China, becoming an option after the 2005 People's Bank of China and China Bank Regulatory Commission administrative ruling for the Credit Asset Securitisation Program. While the global financial crisis has slowed down the development of asset securitisation in China, there has recently been a strong policy drive to develop an ABS market. In 2014, there were three types of asset securitisation products in China; however, they were still relatively small in terms of yearly issuance (Ernst & Young, 2014):

1. credit asset securitisation in the national interbank bond market
2. asset securitisation of securities companies
3. asset-backed notes.

The collateralised loan obligation market saw USD 52 billion of issuance in 2014, with the most active issuer being China Development Bank, whose loans mainly support infrastructure projects. These CLOs have mostly been repackaged railway construction loans with 86% of the assets backing CLOs cited as corporate loans (Wildau, 2015b). Thus, a large proportion of ABS issuance in the renewables, energy efficiency and LEV sectors are likely to come from CLOs. These instruments allow the large banking sector in China to move some of its assets into the broader capital markets. The current policy push to reduce reliance on the banking sector in China could hasten the development of an ABS market and bond markets in general. As such, efforts to support green securitisation should be undertaken in a prudent, judicious and transparent manner so that green ABS markets emerge with integrity and sound financial governance, and with due consideration for any financial stability issues. Limits on banking sector balance sheet capacity in China may lead to changes in financial markets, and could create a higher reliance on the bond market by both municipal borrowers and by corporates who currently rely on the market for syndicated loans from banks and state-owned enterprises.

Based on the prominent role that they play currently domestically, SSA actors could be an important driver of Chinese bond market growth, including for low-carbon bonds. International financial institutions, and Chinese sub-sovereign development banks working in conjunction with policy banks, have the potential to play a pivotal role in the early development of a green bond market in China. Municipal bond issuance is currently low given the traditional reliance of municipalities on bank loans. This is changing rapidly, however, due to government policy aimed at swapping municipal debt for bonds. In 2015, the Chinese government imposed a USD 160 billion quota on banks for loan to municipal bond swaps (Wildau, 2015a).

Japan

Results for Japan show a low degree of securitisation but similar levels of other bond issuance. Investment needs in general are lower compared to the other three markets due to the scale of the economy and nature of the energy transition needed. The equity portion is seen as remaining large, as a high proportion of vehicle purchase is self-financed and is assumed to continue as such. The investment needs over the entire 2015-35 period are estimated by the IEA (2015) to be USD 1.95 trillion.

Figure 3.16. **Annual investment, financing and bond issuance potential in China by 2020**

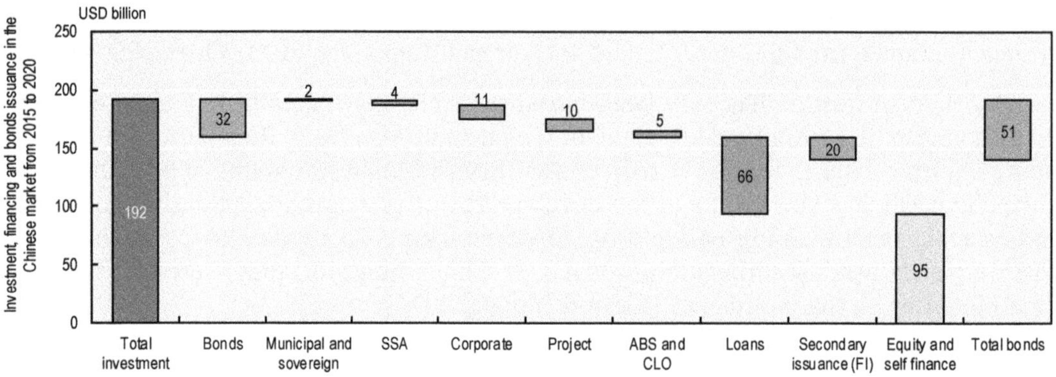

Notes: SSA: supranational, sub-sovereign and agency; ABS = asset-backed security; CLO = collateralised loan obligation.

The baseline scenario suggests that equity can account for 55% through to 2020, rising to 62% in 2035, while the debt portion is lower for Japan compared to the other three regions (60% in the United States, EU and China compared to 40% in Japan). Bond issuance is seen as lower as well, at 23% of overall investment in 2015, decreasing further in 2035 to 19%. This is in contrast to the United States, EU and China where the bond portion accounts for 28-32% of total investment. Yet the amount of low-carbon bonds outstanding is non-trivial, with potential to grow from around USD 25 billion in 2020 to over USD 260 billion in 2035, roughly double the size of the entire labelled green bond market globally in 2015.

In contrast to the other three bond markets, Japan's market is not expected to be dominated by ABS and CLO issuances since the assumed securitisation rate is significantly lower in Japan, reflecting current practice. On the other hand, financial sector and corporate issuance have the potential to account for the largest share of total bonds outstanding throughout the 2015-35 period, reflecting the large Japanese banking and corporate sectors.

Detailed results by physical asset sector

The 2DS investment requirements suggest that by 2035 there could be scope for almost USD 100 billion and USD 65 billion in bonds issued annually by the renewables and energy efficiency sector respectively, while USD 230 billion could be issued to finance LEVs.[24] Between 2015 and 2035, the potential contribution of bonds to the financing of renewable energy is the highest of the three sectors, 34% on average. Bonds contribute only 16% to the financing of energy efficiency projects and 14% to the financing of LEVs. The low rate of bond finance for LEVs is due to high assumed proportions of self-finance in Japan and low securitisation rates used in the models. This reflects the higher capital cost today of LEVs compared to conventional vehicles and the wealthier customer base. Estimating the share of bond financing for the purposes of raising upfront capital and for refinancing investment, and the time lags over which this might occur, is beyond the scope of this analysis but would be very useful to examine.

Figure 3.17. **Annual investment, financing and bond issuance potential in Japan by 2020**

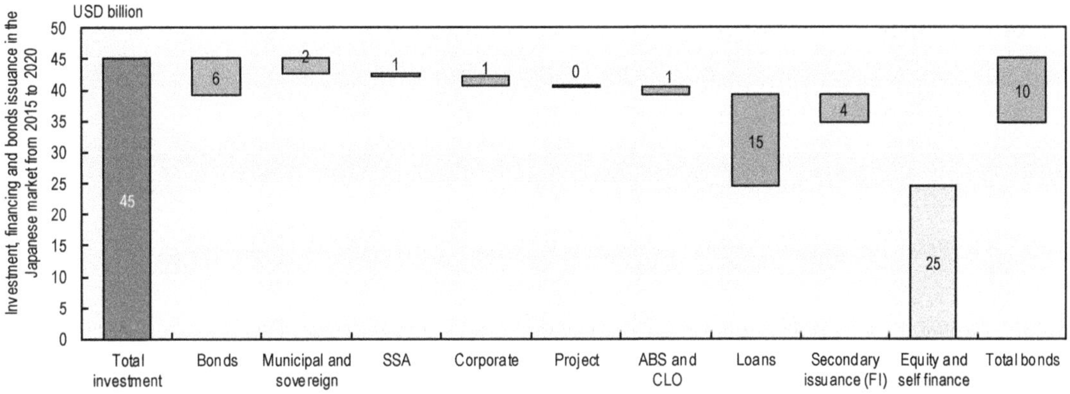

Notes: SSA: supranational, sub-sovereign and agency; ABS = asset-backed security; CLO = collateralised loan obligation.

As LEVs become more affordable, debt financing rates could rise, but no robust assumptions were available to model this scenario. The same is true for any future automotive business model evolutions that could impact on investment needs in the sector (i.e. shared mobility – for example, car sharing and e-hailing). The aggregate investment needs could change as IEA input figures (IEA, 2015) are updated to reflect emerging trends and new policy goals (and as assumptions on the nature of these changes become available). This issue is discussed further below. The difference in the potential role of bonds in the three sectors is partly due to the different roles played by debt finance overall, which is larger for renewable energy, at 75%, than for energy efficiency or low-emission vehicles, around 53%.

However, the financing needs of the LEV sector are so large by comparison to other sectors that its issuance of bonds as modelled significantly exceeds that of other sectors. Of the investment needs in renewable energy, energy efficiency and LEVs, approximately 70% of investments will need to be made in electric and hybrid vehicles between 2015 and 2035 according to the IEA.[25] Consequently, of the USD 392 billion potential annual issuance in 2035, 64% is for LEVs.

Low-emission vehicle financing and bonds

Rates of vehicle financing through leases and loans vary significantly by country and by type of vehicle and owner, whether commercial or passenger. In Germany for instance, 87% of commercial vehicles and 64% of passenger vehicles are leased or financed through loans (with the remainder purchased with cash). A relatively new concept is to lease electric vehicle batteries under a separate contract given degrees of uncertainty over battery lifetimes and high costs of batteries themselves. The rate of securitisation of vehicle purchasing is between 0% and 20% across the world. Assumptions used for the financing of vehicles through bonds, ABS and collateralised debt obligations are conservative. Vehicle purchase financing for the household sector in China is still at an early stage of development, but is growing rapidly. At present, the largest market for auto loan securitisation is in the United States, where it is estimated to represent the potential for around USD 95 billion of annual ABS issuance, but this still only represents 20% of vehicle expenditure in the United States.

The securitisation rate in the EU market is lower still, at 12% of European expenditure on vehicles. Given the high capital cost and low operating costs of LEVs compared to conventional vehicles, credit could become a more prominent method of financing vehicle purchases, either for the whole vehicle, or for the battery pack alone. The introduction of autonomous vehicles and vehicle-sharing business models would increase the importance of credit even further. In the scenarios presented in this analysis, there is some increase in the proportion of vehicle investment which is bond financed, but no disruptive changes have been accommodated.

Figure 3.18. **Potential annual issuance volumes and shares, by physical asset sector, 2020 and 2035**

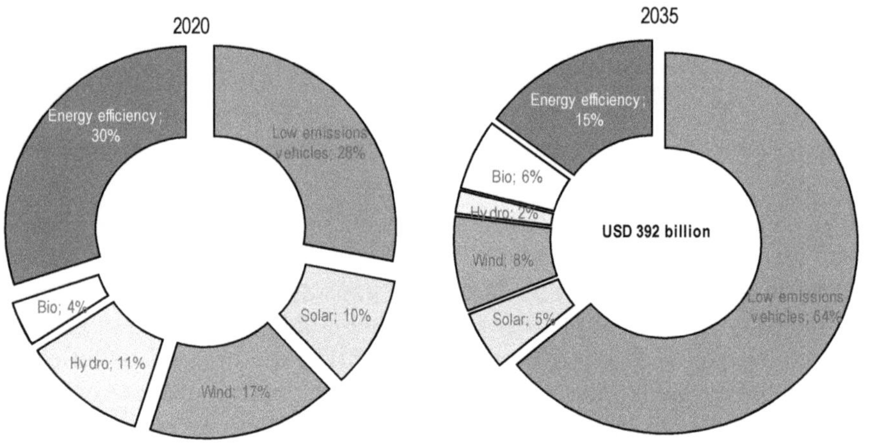

Note: Figures are annual and exclude financial sector issuance where proceeds are allocated to multiple sectors.

Conservative assumptions were used in the model due to uncertainties particular to LEVs. The rate of LEV adoption and the financing and ownership models may change substantially through the 2020s as volumes and ownership take off. As of April 2016, market forecasts and sales figures were already starting to diverge, significantly in some cases (Tesla, 2016; BNEF, 2016). Furthermore, very large changes are conceivable, arising from the adoption of autonomous vehicles, combined with urbanisation and the rise of "on-demand mobility services" (i.e. Zipcar, Uber, Lyft) leading to a potential disruptive switch from personal to fleet ownership, which would imply a much larger role for finance, but at a lower volume of vehicle sales. As such, ABS issuance and bond issuance generally, has possibly very significant upside potential compared to the view taken in the model. Given these uncertainties on how the vehicle market will develop, conservative assumptions were adopted to err on the side of under-calculating potential for future bond issuance.

Renewable energy bonds

Within the renewable energy segment, wind energy appears to have the potential for twice as much bond issuance as solar PV. As is shown in Figure 3.19, aggregate bonds outstanding from solar PV have the potential to reach USD 265 billion in 2035 with annual issuance of around USD 20 billion, while as shown in Figure 3.21, the potential for bonds to finance wind deployment is estimated at over USD 590 billion outstanding in 2035, with annual issuance of around USD 40 billion. Annual bond issuances in the wind sector could experience a boom around the year 2020, as the technology reaches a level of maturity and standardisation which enable it to be suitable for off-balance sheet bond financing. This result stems from a combination of increasing investment in the wind power sector as it becomes less subsidy-reliant and more dependent on market forces, and stronger penetration of bond finance.

Figure 3.19. **Bonds financing solar assets: Issuance and amount outstanding**

USD billion

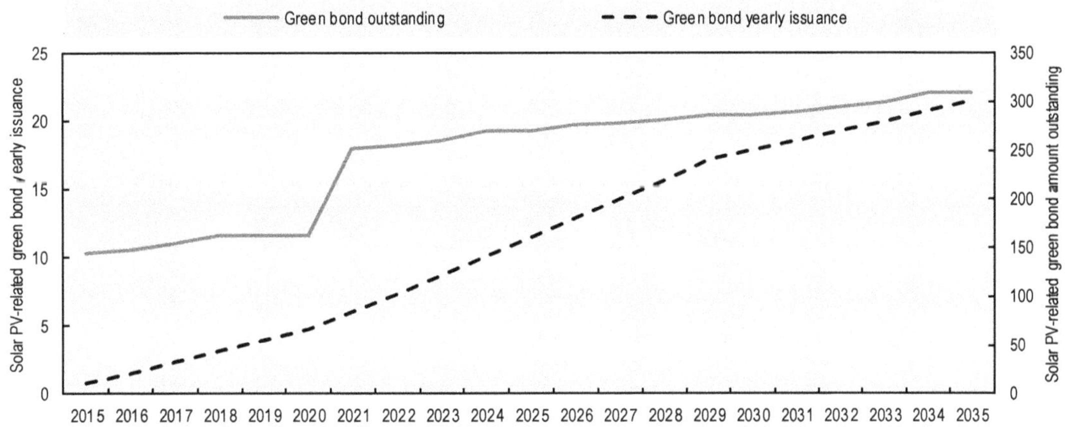

Solar PV may follow suit, creating the circumstances to make the 2020s the "golden years" of renewable energy bond finance. The potential for solar PV figures are smaller than those for wind due to fairly conservative current securitisation assumptions which have been drawn from the literature. Nevertheless, the residential and commercial solar PV sectors have the potential for very high levels of standardisation that leads to a much higher level of securitisation. As of January 2016, there was already evidence of this type of asset securitisation by companies such as SolarCity.

Advocates of distributed solar securitisation argue that smaller deal sizes and fairly simple technology and permitting leads distributed small-scale solar to be a strong candidate for bond financing, with loan portfolios exhibiting risk diversification similar to mortgage backed securities (MBS), and very low idiosyncratic risk. This leads to very substantial upside potential for solar PV ABS, and could be modelled as such if assumptions and data on future securitisation rates can be refined. Aside from photovoltaics, too few assumptions (i.e. from existing practices) on financing structures were available to examine the potential for bond issuance from solar thermal (a technology at an earlier stage of commercialisation). Nonetheless, this sector is projected by the IEA (2014: 45) to require USD 800 billion in capital over the period and could hold potential for bond issuance as well. These levels of investment will, however, only come to pass if the associated deployment levels are enabled through sustained research, development and demonstration.

Implications for institutional investors

Bond finance has the potential to play a significant role in mobilising additional institutional investors to support the low-carbon investment necessary to meet a 2DS by mid-century. However, bond issuance must occur at a scale, and in a format, that such investors are able to absorb. Other sources of potential bond demand exist, such as retail investors, banks and corporations. However, as institutional investor demand has driven the growth of the market to date, it is assumed that this condition would have to endure in order for much higher levels of issuance to be reached (see Chapter 2 and OECD et al. [2016] for a discussion, barriers and policy options for mobilising institutional investors).

Figure 3.20. **Annual and cumulative green ABS/MBS issuance**

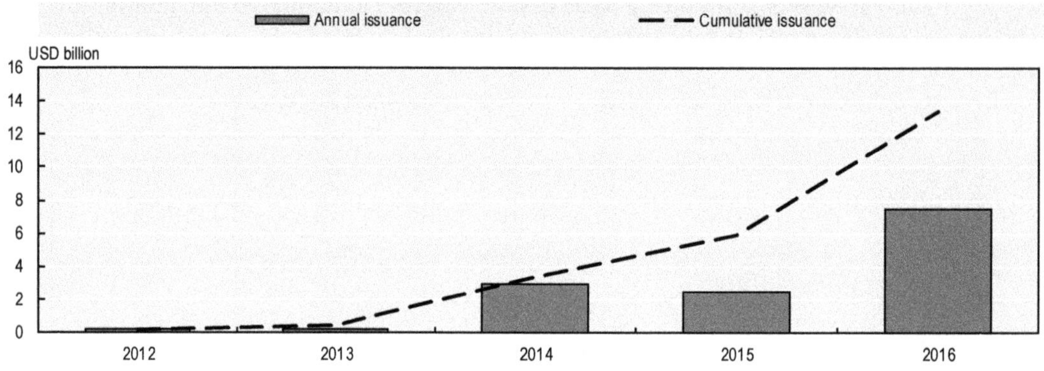

Source: SEB analysis based on Bloomberg (BNEF) data

Figure 3.21. **Bonds financing wind assets: Issuance and amount outstanding**

USD billion

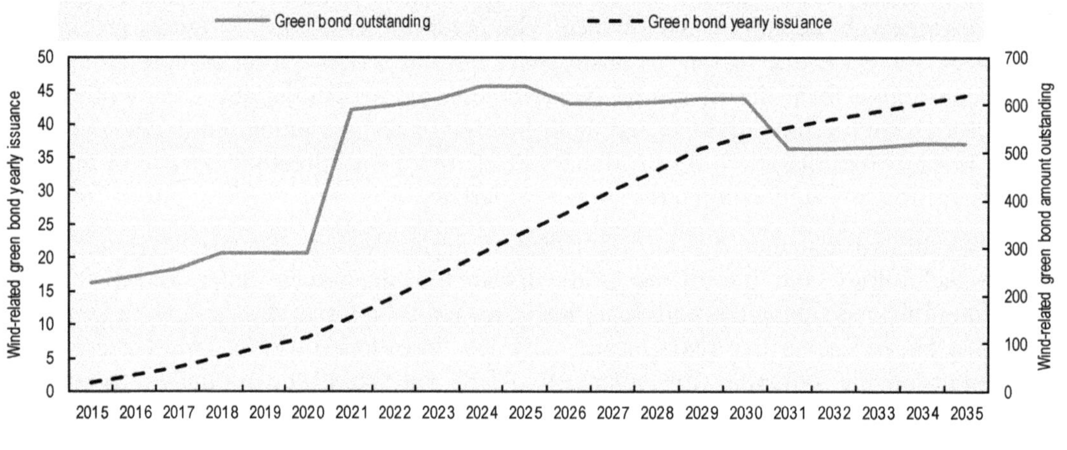

Implications for asset allocation

The following analysis uses data and projections on institutional investor assets under management (AuM) to 2035 to assess the potential scale of low-carbon bonds outstanding, relative to total AuM and bond holdings of the three main types of institutional investors, namely pension funds, insurance companies and investment funds. The results suggest that institutional investors in the OECD have the potential to absorb the increased supply of bonds, through shifting asset allocations in response to the increased percentage of low-carbon bonds as a share of the broader bond markets. This conclusion is based on two assumptions: 1) institutional investors have driven the green bond market growth to date and have shown appetite for low-carbon bonds more generally – this may be expected to grow in light of increasing attention on climate risks and opportunities in investment portfolios; and 2) as institutional investors tend to adopt and reflect broader market trends (given their share of the market), it is reasonable to conclude that they will shift allocations to reflect the increasing share of low-carbon bonds in the market as a whole.

Institutional AuM is projected to grow to over USD 120 trillion in 2019 (OECD, 2015b). Using a projection based on average growth rates adjusted for inflation, institutional AuM could be seen to grow to over USD 190 trillion by 2035. Weighted average allocation to bonds varies significantly by type of investor, with insurance companies allocating 50% to bonds, investment funds 36% and pension funds 24%. As shown in Figure 3.22, institutional investors would need to allocate between 2.5% of assets in the base case and 2.8% in a high securitisation scenario to absorb the bond supply covered in this analysis in 2035. Correspondingly, within the fixed income bond allocations of institutional investors, these low-carbon bonds would account for 6.6-7.3%. The analysis suggests that as these asset categories develop and mature as a share of the broader market, allocations could plateau in the late 2020s.

Figure 3.22. **OECD institutional investor asset allocation to low-carbon bonds as modelled under the base case scenario**

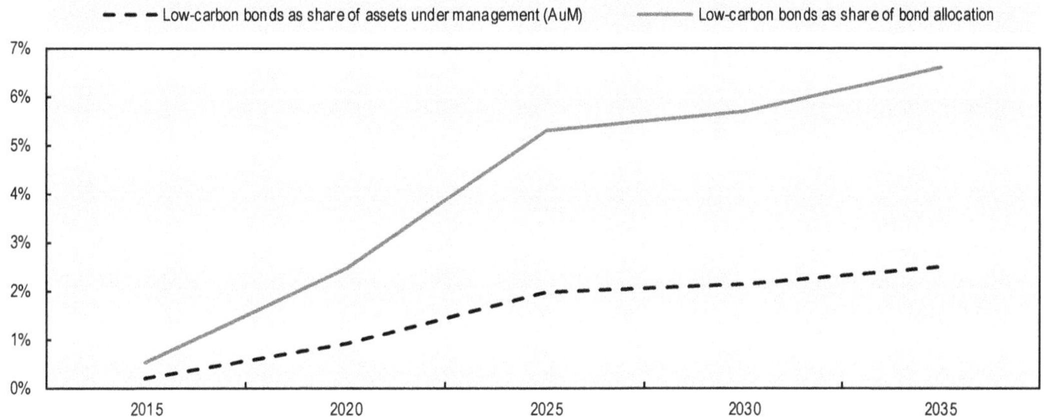

Source: Asset allocation statistics drawn from OECD *Institutional Investor Database*.

The OECD has started to collect data on green bond investments and allocations in its annual Large Pension Fund Survey (OECD, 2016b). As context and as shown in Table 3.2, a noteworthy trend amongst the funds that reported green investments was a general increase in the number of pension funds that invest in green bonds, and also in the relative size of their allocations. Four funds based in Sweden (Alecta, AP2, AP3 and AP4) all increased allocations to green bonds in 2014. Santander, based in Spain, reported green bond exposure for the first time in 2015, amounting to 1.1% of the total portfolio. AP2 and AP3 allocated 1.1% and 1.3% of their portfolios to green bonds, respectively. Note that these allocation figures can be assumed to underrepresent the exposure of these pension funds to the type of bonds discussed in this analysis, as they are allocations to labelled green bonds, and not to other "low-carbon" bonds that could be eligible for a green label.

Mapping channels for institutional investment in green bonds

Green bonds, including the low-carbon bonds examined in this analysis, appeal to institutional investors for a number of reasons as discussed in OECD (2016c; 2015a) and OECD et al. (2016). They also offer the option to access low-carbon investments across a wide variety of channels and asset allocations. The OECD's *Mapping Channels to*

Mobilise Institutional Investment in Sustainable Energy (OECD, 2015a) introduced a "matrix frame" (updated and configured to show green bonds in Figure 3.23), which visualises a range of channels (boxes A-H) that represent typical choices institutional investors need to make when allocating capital to low-carbon investments. Institutional investors consider equity and debt opportunities through a series of lenses (composed of basic investment characteristics).

Table 3.2. **Green investments of select large pension funds and public pension reserve funds, 2014**

% of total investments

Country head office	Name of the fund or institution	Total investments in 2014 (USD million)	Green investments (as a % of total investments)				
			Green equity	Green bonds	Alternative green asset classes[1]	Other green investments	Total green investments
Australia	Health Employees Superannuation Trust Australia[2]	25 030	..	..	0.3	..	0.3
Brazil	FAPES - BNDES	3 189	0.2	..	..	..	0.2
	Previ[3]	62 733	..	..	..	0.1	0.1
Denmark	PFA Pension	46 075	0.4	..	0.3	..	0.7
Finland	Valtion Eläkerahasto	21 378	..	..	0.3	..	0.3
France	ERAFP[4]	25 587	24.7	0.0	..	..	24.7
Netherlands	PFZW	196 333	1.4	0.5	0.4	0.5	2.8
	PMT	71 112	..	..	0.1	..	0.1
	Stichting Pensioenfonds ABP[5]	473 569	1.5	0.3	0.8	4.0	6.7
New Zealand	New Zealand Superannuation Fund[6]	21 473	..	..	0.0	6.7	6.7
Norway	Government Pension Fund – Global	872 607	..	..	..	0.6	0.6
Romania	Azt Viitorul Tau	1 152	..	..	..	0.2	0.2
Spain	Endesa	1 923	..	0.2	..	..	0.2
	Fonditel[7]	3 972	1.2	..	0.1	..	1.3
	Santander[8]	205	..	1.1	..	..	1.1
Sweden	Alecta	88 330	..	0.3	..	..	0.3
	AP2[6]	37 990	1.1	1.1	4.3	2.5	9.0
	AP3	37 271	..	1.3	0.0	0.0	1.3
	AP4	38 124	..	0.6	..	..	0.6
United Kingdom	USS[9]	62 972	..	..	0.3	0.1	0.4
United States	New York City Combined Retirement System	159 189	0.3	..	..	..	0.3
	United Nations Joint Staff Pension Fund	52 821	0.3	0.2	..	..	0.4

Notes: Some funds have green investments (in "green" indices for instance) but cannot separate these investments from other portfolio investments, as is the case for Keva in Finland, and Illinois SURS in the United States (green private equity).

... Not available.

1. The alternative green asset classes include hedge funds, natural resources, private equity, infrastructure and inflation-linked bonds. 2. Includes investment in private equity clean technology. 3. Green investments are defined by Previ as assets (such as stocks, exchange-traded funds and mutual funds) in which the underlying business(es) are somehow involved in operations aimed at improving the environment. 4. If investments based on the FTSE4Good or similar methodologies are considered as green investments, all the investments in equity by ERAFP could be seen as green, since ERAFP applied an environment, social and governance (ESG) best-in-class approach to all the equity mandates. 5. Other investments include green real estate, which are defined as properties with a GreenStar label in the Global Real Estate Sustainability Benchmark Index, and that have an above-average performance on sustainability. 6. Other investments include forestry. 7. Data refer to Fonditel's biggest pension plan: Empleados de Telefónica de España. 8. Reported values are as of 30 September 2015. 9. Other green investments include renewable and lower carbon infrastructure, cleantech private equity and a listed environmental technology fund.

Source: OECD calculations based on responses to the OECD Survey of Large Pension Funds and Public Pension Reserve Funds.

A first choice is whether the exposure desired is to projects, corporates or both. Institutional investors can make green bond investments directly ("in-house") if they have the capability to do so, or they can outsource these investments via an "intermediated" channel such as a fund. Investments can be made on a listed or unlisted basis. Green bonds can theoretically be classified into each of these channels (Figure 3.23); in practice, however, a lack of publicly available information leads to certain channels appearing unoccupied in the figure (e.g. while institutional investors anecdotally invest in privately placed corporate bonds, no public record is currently available).

Figure 3.23. **A "matrix frame" to map channels for institutional investment in green bonds**

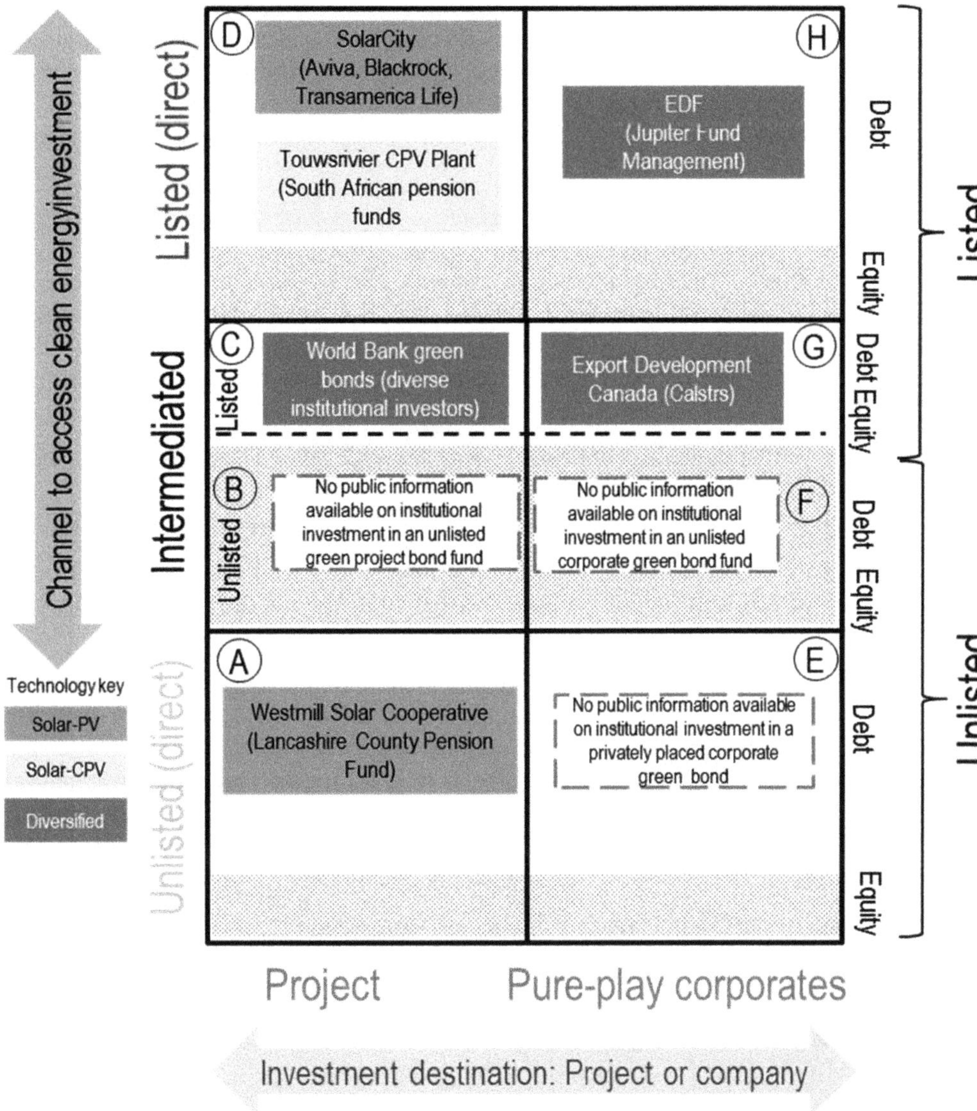

Notes: Coloured boxes are examples of green bond investments by selected institutional investors (named in brackets where information is publicly available – bonds will have more than these listed investors). Annex 3.A4 gives details on the bonds. Colours represent technologies. Although not shown here, diversified corporates can also issue a green bond where the proceeds are reserved for "green projects or activities. "Pure-play" refers to entities focused on only one industry or product, e.g. a solar PV company.

Source: OECD analysis based on methodology laid out in OECD (2015a).

Notes

1. The IEA *World Energy Outlook* "450 Scenario" sets out an energy pathway consistent with the goal of limiting the global increase in temperature to 2°C by limiting the concentration of greenhouse gases in the atmosphere to around 450 parts per million of CO_2. The 2°C Scenario (2DS) is the focus of the IEA's *Energy Technology Perspectives*. The 2DS describes an energy system consistent with an emissions trajectory that recent climate science research indicates would give an 80% chance of limiting average global temperature increase to 2°C. It sets the target of cutting energy-related CO_2 emissions by more than half in 2050 (compared with 2009) and ensuring that they continue to fall thereafter. The 2DS acknowledges that transforming the energy sector is vital, but not the sole solution: the goal can only be achieved if CO_2 and greenhouse gas emissions in non-energy sectors are also reduced. The 2DS is broadly consistent with the *World Energy Outlook* 450 Scenario through 2035 (*Source:* IEA, 2014; 2015).

2. At COP21 Parties agreed to hold the increase in the global average temperature to "well below 2°C and pursue efforts to limit the temperature increase to 1.5°C above pre-industrial levels". Corresponding investment needs figures had not been estimated by the IEA by the time this research commenced. However, more stringent mitigation scenarios are likely to require more early investments in lower emissions technologies, and when these figures become available, the model could analyse them in the same way as for a 2DS.

3. Low-emissions vehicles are defined as plug-in and electric vehicles, fuel cell and hybrid vehicles with emissions of less than 90 gCO_2/km, in line with the IEA *Energy Technology Perspectives* (2012) total transport investment needs figures for a 2DS.

4. If sufficiently granular data and assumptions were to be made available, the framework constructed for the purposes of this analysis could in theory be applied to these other sectors as well.

5. With increasingly clearer understandings of the economic benefits of the green label being applied to bonds (as discussed in OECD et al. [2016]), it may be reasonable to assume that the percentage of bonds labelled as green would increase in the future. For example, recent public sector-led efforts to grow a green labelled bond market in China and India suggest that in those markets, at the very least, the percentage of bonds potentially eligible for carrying a green label will be higher in the future than at present.

6. By the end of 2015, outstanding bonds in China amounted to RMB 47.9 trillion (USD 7.4 trillion). Gross bond issuance in China in 2015 amounted to USD 3.4 trillion (Source: PBOC).

7. Gross issuance. OECD analysis based on IEA (2014, 2012), Climate Bonds Initiative, BIS, SIFMA, ECB, JSRI, ADB and Goldman Sachs data.

8. Due to the skew in investment needs caused by the dominance of the LEV sector in IEA figures and in these composite results, these investment needs may appear to diverge from some recent Chinese estimates for overall green investment (e.g. CCICED, 2015), which show that needs will peak in the next 5-15 years, and may decline after 2030. Further comparisons of LEV sector assumptions would be useful to undertake here in this respect.

9. Without more granular precision on the future evolution in China, a conservative assumption is used.

10. Note that while the model generates results down to the decimal place as a result of its calibrations, figures are rounded up in the discursive analysis to reflect the inherent uncertainties commensurate with technological, product and financial market evolutions over the next 20 years.

11. OECD analysis based on data from BIS, SIFMA, ECB, JSRI, ADB and Goldman Sachs.

12. As described by Dewar (2011), accessing the capital markets to fund projects and infrastructure arguably dates to the 1800s with the US railroad expansion. The first modern private sector project bond offerings date to the 1980s and early 1990s, encouraged in part by changes in the US securities regulatory regime that facilitated bond offerings to institutional investors. The first wave of project bonds financed or refinanced independent power projects and quickly evolved to a broad range of electric, oil and gas, water and other power-related assets; as well as toll roads, railways, and eventually social infrastructure such as hospitals, schools and prisons.

13. Note that while the model generates results down to the decimal place as a result of its calibrations, figures are rounded up in the discursive analysis to reflect the inherent uncertainties commensurate with technological, product and financial market evolutions over the next 20 years.

14. As defined by the Green Bond Principles, see: www.icmagroup.org/Regulatory-Policy-and-Market-Practice/green-bonds/green-bond-principles.

15. From a high-level perspective, as a means of efficiently channelling financial and economic resources, securitisation supports economic growth and financial stability by enabling issuers and investors to diversify risk. By opening up new avenues for raising capital, securitisation can aid in diversifying the funding base of the economy. Securitisation can also help free up bank capital, which in theory allows banks to extend new credit to the economy (Source: Segoviano et al., 2015).

16. For instance, the European Commission's Securitisation Regulation will apply to all securitisations in the EU and include due diligence, risk retention and transparency rules together with the criteria for simple, transparent and standardised ("STS") securitisations. This is accompanied by a proposal to amend the EU Capital Requirements Regulation to make the capital treatment of securitisations for banks and investment firms more risk-sensitive and able to reflect properly the specific features of STS securitisations.

17. The US National Renewable Energy Laboratory (NREL) Solar Access to Public Capital (SAPC) Working Group was designed to open capital market investment for solar assets via securitisation and other financial innovations. The SAPC was a three-year initiative that ended in September 2015. SAPC membership included over 440 organisations such as top residential and commercial solar developers, law firms, investment banks and capital managers, rating agencies, independent engineers, and other key stakeholders in the solar finance space.

18. i.e. limits on the amount of debt these entities can take on directly before risking a credit rating downgrade.

19. It should be noted that, in many jurisdictions, the attractiveness of financing via project bonds is affected by competition from the project finance bank lending and "term loan B" or mezzanine debt markets. Constructing a sensitivity analysis to

address these issues was not possible due to lack of credible assumptions, but these factors could negatively or positively affect the potential for project bond financing shown in the analysis.

20. CLOs are ABS securities that consist of a portfolio of different loans.

21. According to SIFMA, the amount outstanding of agency and non-agency residential MBS is USD 8 trillion, while the Federal Reserve Financial Accounts statistics report a figure of USD 13 trillion for residential mortgage debt outstanding.

22. SIFMA reports a figure of close to USD 100 billion in 2014 for the outstanding amount of auto loan ABS, while the aggregate expenditure on new vehicles stood at USD 450 billion.

23. The analysis of the potential for bond financing in other emerging market countries is beyond the scope of this analysis and would require enhanced data and assumptions to be made available for a rigorous assessment to be attempted. However, the results of the analysis of China's scenarios for bond market financing in a 2DS coupled with the similar investment needs profiles of other major emerging markets suggests that other emerging markets could follow a similar low-carbon bond financing trajectory, if governments implement policies to get on a low-carbon pathway, but with a delay of five to ten years due to differing stages of financial market development and accompanying policy efforts.

24. Excluding the USD 230 billion in annual financial sector issuance (where proceeds are allocated to multiple sectors).

25. This investment reflects the financing cost of the vehicle incurred by end users – enabling infrastructure such as charging stations is excluded.

References

Bielenberg, A. et al. (2016), "Financing change: How to mobilize private sector financing for sustainable infrastructure", McKinsey & Company Center for Business and Environment, January, http://newclimateeconomy.report/2015/wp-content/uploads/sites/3/2016/01/Financing_change_How_to_mobilize_private-sector_financing_for_sustainable-_infrastructure.pdf.

BNEF (2016), "Electric vehicles to be 35% of global new car sales by 2040", press release, Bloomberg New Energy Finance, 25 February, http://about.bnef.com/press-releases/electric-vehicles-to-be-35-of-global-new-car-sales-by-2040.

CBI/HSBC (2015), "Bonds and climate change: The state of the market in 2016", Climate Bonds Initiative and HSBC, July, www.climatebonds.net/files/files/CBI%20State%20of%20the%20Market%202016%20A4.pdf.

CBI/LSE (2015), "Green Securitisation Roundtable: A public sector agenda for green securitisation market development in Europe", discussion paper, 8 June, Climate Bonds Initiative and London School of Economics, https://www.climatebonds.net/files

/files/Discussion%20primer%20Green%20Securitization%20Roundtable%208%20June.pdf.

CCICED (2015), *China: Green Finance and Green Transformation*, China Council for International Cooperation on Environment and Development.

Dewar, J. (2011), *International Project Finance: Law and Practice*, Oxford University Press, New York.

EC (2016), "Securitisation initiative", European Commission, http://ec.europa.eu/finance/securities/securitisation/index_en.htm#maincontentSec1.

ECB (2015), "Consolidated banking data" (database), *ECB Statistical Data Warehouse.*

Ehlers, T. (2014), "Understanding the challenges for infrastructure finance", *BIS Working Papers*, No. 454, Bank for International Settlements, August, www.bis.org/publ/work454.pdf.

Ehlers, T., F. Packer and E. Remolona (2014), "Infrastructure and corporate bond markets in Asia", Conference Volume, Reserve Bank of Australia, www.rba.gov.au/publications/confs/2014/pdf/ehlers-packer-remolona.pdf.

Ernst & Young (2014), "EY insights : Securitization in China", Ernst & Young (China), www.ey.com/Publication/vwLUAssets/EY-Securitization-in-China-en/$FILE/EY-Securitization-in-China-en.pdf.

IEA (2015), *Energy Technology Perspectives 2015*, OECD Publishing, Paris, http://dx.doi.org/10.1787/energy_tech-2015-en.

IEA (2014), *World Energy Investment Outlook*, OECD/IEA Publishing, Paris, www.iea.org/publications/freepublications/publication/WEIO2014.pdf.

IEA (2012), *Energy Technology Perspectives 2012: Pathways to a Clean Energy System*, OECD Publishing, Paris, http://dx.doi.org/10.1787/energy_tech-2012-en.

Lowder, T. and M. Mendelsohn (2013), *The Potential of Securitization in Solar PV Finance*, Report by the National Renewable Energy Laboratory (NREL), www.nrel.gov/docs/fy14osti/60230.pdf.

OECD (2016a), *Green Investment Banks: Scaling up Private Investment in Low-carbon, Climate-resilient Infrastructure*, OECD Publishing, Paris, http://dx.doi.org/10.1787/9789264245129-en.

OECD (2016b), "Annual Survey of Large Pension Funds and Public Pension Reserve Funds: Report on pension funds' long-term investments", OECD, Paris, www.oecd.org/daf/fin/privatepensions/2015-Large-Pension-Funds-Survey.pdf.

OECD (2016c), "Progress report on approaches to mobilising institutional investment for green infrastructure", OECD, Paris, http://unepinquiry.org/wp-content/uploads/2016/09/11_Progress_Report_on_Approaches_to_Mobilising_Institutional_Investment_for_Green_Infrastructure.pdf.

OECD (2015a), *Mapping Channels to Mobilise Institutional Investment in Sustainable Energy*, OECD Publishing, Paris, http://dx.doi.org/10.1787/9789264224582-en

OECD (2015b), *OECD Business and Finance Outlook 2015*, OECD Publishing, Paris, http://dx.doi.org/10.1787/9789264234291-en.

OECD et al. (2016) "Green bonds: Country experiences, barriers and options", OECD/ICMA/CBI/China GFC, http://unepinquiry.org/wp-content/uploads/2016/09/6_Green_Bonds_Country_Experiences_Barriers_and_Options.pdf.

PBoC/UNEP (2015), "Establishing China's green financial system", Final Report to the Green Finance Task Force, People's Bank of China and United Nations Environment Programme, April, www.cbd.int/financial/privatesector/china-Green%20Task%20Force%20Report.pdf.

Segoviano, M. et al. (2015), "Securitization: The road ahead", *Staff Discussion Note*, International Monetary Fund, Washington, DC, www.imf.org/external/pubs/ft/sdn/2015/sdn1501.pdf.

SIFMA (2015), *US Bond Market Issuance and Outstanding* (database), www.sifma.org/research/statistics.aspx.

Standard & Poor's Ratings Services (2014), *Credit Shift: As Global Corporate Borrowers Seek $60 Trillion, Asia-Pacific Debt Will Overtake U.S. And Europe Combined*, www.finyear.com/attachment/498696.

Tesla (2016), "Tesla delivers 14,820 vehicles in Q1 2016", press release, 4 April, Tesla Motors, http://ir.teslamotors.com/releasedetail.cfm?ReleaseID=963460.

US DOE/NREL (2015), Solar Access to Public Capital, webpage, https://financere.nrel.gov/finance/content/solar-securitization-and-solar-access-public-capital-sapc-working-group.

Wildau, G. (2015a), "Sliced and diced loans take off in China", *The Financial Times*, 19 February.

Wildau, G. (2015b), "China imposes $160bn municipal bonds for debt swap", *The Financial Times*, 13 May, https://www.ft.com/content/28bc38a6-f920-11e4-8e16-00144feab7de.

Annex 3.A1.
Methodology, model structure, assumptions and sources for capital structure data

The analysis aims to decompose the International Energy Agency's (IEA) investment figures sequentially by sector, sub-sector, investor, project type and type of finance. Investment data are sourced from the IEA *World Energy Investment Outlook* (2014), where the 450 Scenario (see Glossary) was used. When the relevant sectors were not available in the *World Energy Investment Outlook* data, the IEA *Energy Technology Perspectives* (2012) was used. Only aggregated data by sector were available. The investment breakdown is carried out using relevant data found in the IEA reports as well as other sources, including industry reports. When the breakdown is available in the IEA reports, it is usually on a global scale. For example, 55% of solar photovoltaic (PV) investment will be utility scale, while rooftop PV will account for the remaining proportion. This ratio is then applied for all countries in the modelling. It is hoped that a more detailed breakdown of investment data will be available for the 2DS scenarios from both the *World Energy Investment Outlook* and *Energy Technology Perspectives*.

Data on project finance are needed to validate assumptions about the likely breakdown of investment into sources of finance. Currently a global average of project finance structures is used, while relevant adjustments are made to account for different levels of usage of project bonds across regions, where the data are available. The analysis would benefit from regional data on the involvement of international financial institutions, including development banks, which are available from a few data providers including *Thomson Reuters' Project Finance International* database and *IJGlobal* database. Further data on how project finance is structured in different regions are sought-after.

Ehlers, Packer and Remolona (2014) provide data on the share of bonds and syndicated loans in financing infrastructure projects in the power sector in key markets. The level of government and international financial institutions' involvement in project finance was obtained, for the global market, from the IJGlobal *Project Finance Infrastructure Review* (2014).

Typical gearing ratios (the ratio of total debt to total equity) for US utilities was sourced from US financial accounts. The ratio of bond finance-to-debt finance is assumed to be equal to the aggregate ratio for the entire US corporate business sector, which was sourced from both the US financial accounts and S&P data. For EU utilities, firm-level financial accounts were available and used to compute a leverage ratio for the European power sector as well as the ratio of bond-to-debt finance.

The level of debt and bond finance was more challenging to determine for Chinese firms. S&P data show that Chinese corporations have a low bond-to-debt ratio, while project finance data, especially in the power sector, show more substantial reliance on bond finance, as documented by Ehlers, Packer and Remolona (2014). The baseline scenario was constructed using an average of these two ratios.

The corporate financing structure of energy efficiency projects is based on IEA (2014), Standard and Poor's Ratings Services (2014) and IJGlobal (2014).

The green vehicles financing model is based on analysis done by KPMG (2012). The cost of the entire vehicle is published in the IEA's 2012 *Energy Technology Perspectives*. Full cost is the appropriate investment figure in this context as well as for new-build residential and commercial building (data on the latter are currently unavailable). For other energy efficiency investments, only incremental investment is considered.

The rate of asset securitisation is largely based on current market data published by the Securities Industry and Financial Markets Association (SIFMA), the Association for Financial Markets in Europe, and the European Covered Bond Council, in conjunction with data on aggregate expenditure on motor vehicles from national accounts. While estimates and projections are largely absent from the literature, aggregate expenditure has the potential to change dramatically if new business models emerge that substitute for private ownership, offsetting some of the high capital costs.

Since the crash in securitisation in 2007, the rates have varied, but they have been on an upswing since Q3 2015. Auto asset-backed securities have recovered better than expected. A focus has been placed on the implication of different securitisation rates in the scenario analysis. Where data were unavailable, assumptions were constructed to simulate values. Annex 3.A2 contains further numerical detail for assumptions.

Finally, two financing models were considered for rooftop solar PV and distributed wind energy. In the first, third-party ownership, the rate of bond financing is similar to the rate for corporate utilities, albeit issuance is assumed to be in the form of asset-backed securities. In the second, bank loan financing, a proportion of these loans reach the bond market via loan securitisation.

The analysis uses available data, conservative assumptions and acknowledges three important areas of uncertainty: policy, current practice and future changes in practice. First, as illustrated by the range of scenarios which the IEA publishes (in its *World Energy Outlook* and Energy Technology Perspectives models), there is uncertainty in investment caused by uncertainty in the strength of policy adopted and uncertainty in how technology costs and performance will evolve, as well as the mix in which they will be adopted.

Second, there is uncertainty in the current data on financial structures and sources of finance. Some financial markets are better documented than others. Securities regulations generally require that public market transactions be thoroughly and publicly documented – and therefore easier to analyse. A substantial portion of financial market transactions are private, may be unlisted and have limited disclosure of deal specifics. In these cases, third-party market analysis is the only option, rather than primary audited financial reports.

Third, financial practices may change. Although traditional financing structures will certainly continue, waves of financial innovation are often driven by changes in regulation, market preferences, corporate balance sheets, tax structures, financial crises and other factors. The types of financial structures deployed may be profoundly affected by such market shifts. The People's Republic of China's debt markets have experienced challenges and the financial system is undergoing significant change. As such, there are significant uncertainties regarding the future role of bond financing for low-carbon infrastructure. At the same time, the government has prioritised the development of green bond markets (PBoC/UNEP, 2015).

Figure 3.A1.1. **Model structure**

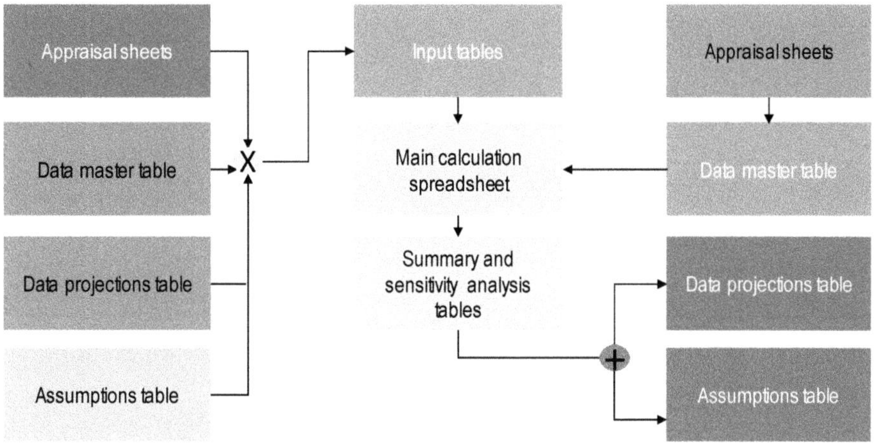

Table 3.A1.1. **Financial products and sources by sector**

Sector	Sub-sector	Investor	Project type	Source of finance
Solar	Solar PV CSP	Utility scale	Project finance Corporate	Equity Syndicated loans Project bonds Corporate bonds International financial institution loans
	Solar PV	Rooftop Household Commercial Public sector		Equity/self-finance Leasing/power purchase agreement Bank loans
Wind	Onshore Offshore	Utility scale	Project finance Corporate	Equity Syndicated loans Project bonds Corporate bonds SSA loans
	Onshore	Distributed/small scale Household Commercial Public sector		Equity/self-finance Leasing/power purchase agreement Bank loans
Hydropower		Utilities Large Small scale	Project finance Corporate	Equity Syndicated loans Project bonds Corporate bonds SSA/government loans
Bioenergy		Utilities Industry Building	Project finance Corporate	Equity Syndicated loans Project bonds Corporate bonds SSA/government loans
Energy efficiency	Energy intensive industries			Equity/self-finance Loans Bonds
	Non-energy intensive industries			Equity/self-finance Loans Bonds
	Transport Electric vehicles Other modes of transport Transport infrastructure	Investors Household Commercial Public sector		Equity/self-finance Loans Bonds
	Buildings Appliances Heating and cooling Insulation Others	Investors Household Commercial Public sector		Equity/self-finance Loans Bonds

Figure 3.A1.2. **Decomposition of investment figures**

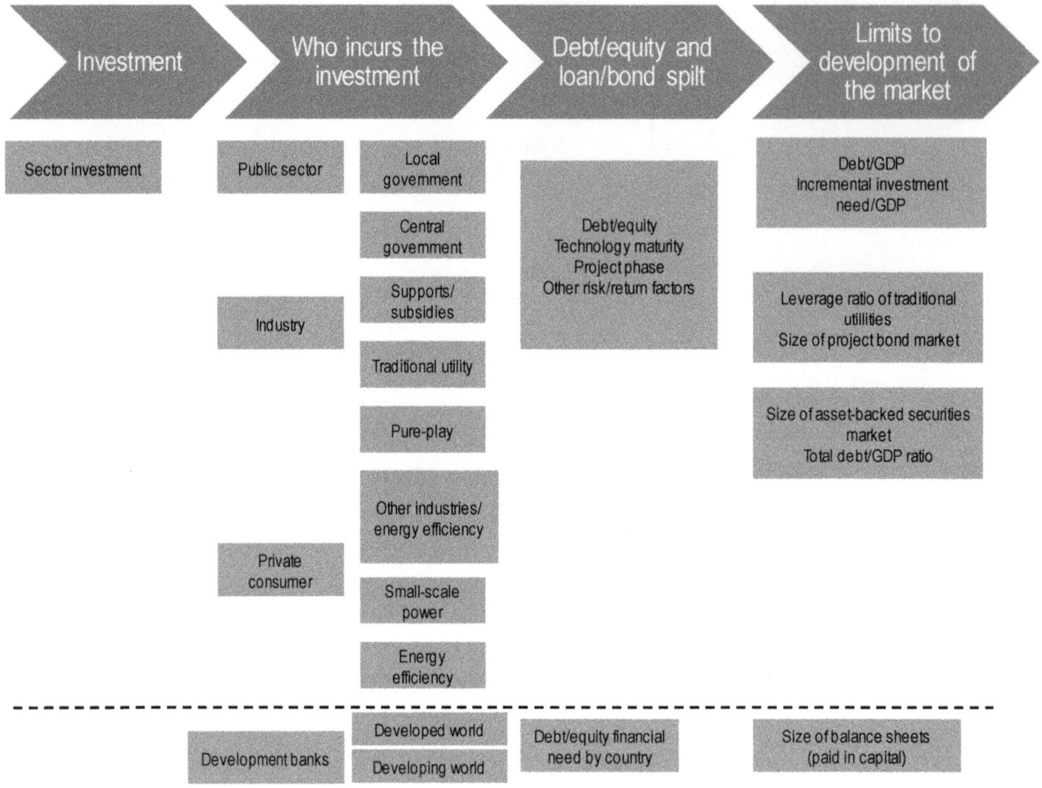

References

Ehlers, T., F. Packer and E. Remolona (2014), "Infrastructure and corporate bond markets in Asia", Conference Volume, Reserve Bank of Australia, www.rba.gov.au/publications/confs/2014/pdf/ehlers-packer-remolona.pdf.

IEA (2014), *World Energy Investment Outlook*, OECD/IEA, Paris, www.iea.org/publications/freepublications/publication/WEIO2014.pdf.

IEA (2012), *Energy Technology Perspectives 2012*, OECD/IEA Publishing, Paris, www.iea.org/publications/freepublications/publication/ETP2012_free.pdf.

IJGlobal (2014), *Project Finance Infrastructure Review*.

KPMG (2012), "Global automotive finance and leasing: The role of product diversification and emerging markets in future growth", KPMG International Cooperative, https://assets.kpmg.com/content/dam/kpmg/pdf/2012/09/automotive-finance-leasing.pdf.

PBoC/UNEP (2015), "Establishing China's green financial system", Final Report to the Green Finance Task Force, People's Bank of China and United Nations Environment Programme, April, www.cbd.int/financial/privatesector/china-Green%20Task%20Force%20Report.pdf.

Standard & Poor's Ratings Services (2014), *Credit Shift: As Global Corporate Borrowers Seek $60 Trillion, Asia-Pacific Debt Will Overtake U.S. And Europe Combined*, www.finyear.com/attachment/498696.

Annex 3.A2.
Financial breakdown assumptions

Table 3.A2.1. **Financial breakdown assumptions: United States**

	Unit	2020	2025	2030	2035
Project finance					
Equity	%	20	20	20	20
Government	%	2	2	2	2
International financial institutions	%	7	7	7	7
Commercial loan	%	61	40	30	20
Bonds	%	5	15	20	30
Securitisation	%	5	15	20	20
Corporate finance					
Equity	%	33	33	33	33
Debt	%	68	68	68	68
Bonds	%	41	41	41	41
Long-term loans	%	27	27	27	27
Loan securitisation	%	10	15	20	20
Bond tenor	Years	15	15	15	15
Rooftop solar PV (financing model)					
Third-party ownership	%	60	60	60	60
Solar loan	%	40	40	40	40
Securitisation levels by types of finance					
Third-party securitisation	%	41	41	41	41
Loan securitisation	%	12	36	36	36
Government financing inputs					
Government leverage ratio in renewable energy	%	80	80	80	80
Government bond-to-loan ratio	%	100	100	100	100
Energy intensive industry					
Equity/self-finance	%	40	40	40	40
Bonds	%	36	36	36	36
Loans	%	19	19	19	19
Non-energy intensive industry					
Equity/self-finance	%	40	40	40	40
Bonds	%	36	36	36	36
Loans	%	19	19	19	19
Green cars					
Households					
Equity/self-finance	%	5	5	5	5
Loans	%	95	95	95	95
Leases	%	0	0	0	0
Commercial					
Equity/self-finance	%	62	62	62	62
Loans	%	17	17	17	17
Buildings, residential					
Households					
Equity/self-finance	%	51	51	51	51
Loans	%	49	49	49	49
Buildings, services					
Commercial					

Table 3.A2.1. **Financial breakdown assumptions: United States** (*continued*)

	Unit	2020	2025	2030	2035
Equity/self-finance	%	51	51	51	51
Bonds	%	25	25	25	25
Loans	%	20	20	20	20
Government					
Equity/self-finance	%	51	51	51	51
Bonds	%	49	49	49	49
Loans	%				
Energy intensive industry					
Loan securitisation	%	10	10	10	10
Non-energy intensive industry					
Loan securitisation	%	10	10	10	10
Green cars					
Loan securitisation	%	35	35	35	35
Buildings, residential					
Loan securitisation	%	36	36	36	36
Buildings, services					
Loan securitisation	%	26	26	26	26

Table 3.A2.2. **Financial breakdown assumptions: European Union**

	Unit	2020	2025	2030	2035
Project finance					
Equity	%	20	20	20	20
Government	%	3	3	3	3
International financial institutions	%	10	10	10	10
Commercial loan	%	58	40	30	20
Bonds	%	4	17	22	32
Securitisation	%	5	10	15	15
Corporate finance					
Equity	%	33	33	33	33
Debt	%	68	68	68	68
Bonds	%	32	32	32	32
Long-term loans	%	36	36	36	36
Loan securitisation	%	10	15	15	15
Bond tenor	Years	15	15	15	15
Rooftop solar PV (financing model)					
Third-party ownership	%	40	0	0	0
Solar loan	%	60	0	0	0
Securitisation levels by types of finance					
Third-party securitisation	%	32	0	0	0
Loan securitisation	%	12	0	0	0
Government financing inputs					
Government leverage ratio in renewable energy	%	80	80	80	80
Government bond-to-loan ratio	%	80	80	80	80
Energy intensive industry					
Equity/self-finance	%	40	40	40	40
Bonds	%	21	21	21	21
Loans	%	29	29	29	29
Non-energy intensive industry					
Equity/self-finance	%	40	40	40	40
Bonds	%	21	21	21	21

Table 3.A2.2. **Financial breakdown assumptions: European Union** (*continued*)

	Unit	2020	2025	2030	2035
Loans	%	29	29	29	29
Green cars					
Households					
Equity/self-finance	%	24	24	24	24
Loans	%	76	76	76	76
Leases	%	0	0	0	0
Commercial					
Equity/self-finance	%	43	43	43	43
Loans	%	35	35	35	35
Buildings, residential					
Households					
Equity/self-finance	%	51	51	51	51
Loans	%	49	49	49	49
Buildings, services					
Commercial					
Equity/self-finance	%	51	51	51	51
Bonds	%	17	17	17	17
Loans	%	22	22	22	22
Government					
Equity/self-finance	%	51	52	53	54
Bonds	%	49	48	47	46
Loans	%	0	0	0	0
Energy intensive industry					
Loan securitisation	%	10	10	10	10
Non-energy intensive industry					
Loan securitisation	%	10	10	10	10
Green cars					
Loan securitisation	%	15	20	20	20
Buildings, residential					
Loan securitisation	%	25	25	25	25
Buildings, services					
Loan securitisation	%	20	20	30	30

Table 3.A2.3. **Financial breakdown assumptions: People's Republic of China**

	Unit	2020	2025	2030	2035
Project finance					
Equity	%	20	20	20	20
Government	%	3	3	3	3
International financial institutions	%	10	10	10	10
Commercial loan	%	20	20	20	20
Bonds	%	42	37	37	37
Securitisation	%	5	10	10	10
Corporate finance					
Equity	%	30	30	30	30
Debt	%	70	70	70	70
Bonds	%	20	20	20	20
Long-term loans	%	50	50	50	50
Loan securitisation	%	0	5	10	10
Bond tenor	Years	15	15	15	15
Rooftop solar PV (financing model)					

Table 3.A2.3. **Financial breakdown assumptions: People's Republic of China** (*continued*)

	Unit	2020	2025	2030	2035
Third-party ownership	%	30	0	0	0
Solar loan	%	70	0	0	0
Securitisation levels by type of finance					
Third-party securitisation	%	20	0	0	0
Loan securitisation	%	0	0	0	0
Government financing inputs					
Government leverage ratio in renewable energy	%	80	80	80	80
Government bond-to-loan ratio	%	10	20	30	40
Energy intensive industry					
Equity/self-finance	%	40	40	40	40
Bonds	%	13	13	13	13
Loans	%	37	37	37	37
Non-energy intensive industry					
Equity/self-finance	%	40	40	40	40
Bonds	%	13	13	13	13
Loans	%	37	37	37	37
Green cars					
Households					
Equity/self-finance	%	70	70	70	70
Loans	%	30	30	30	30
Leases	%	0	0	0	0
Commercial					
Equity/self-finance	%	85	85	85	85
Loans	%	15	15	15	15
Buildings, residential					
Households					
Equity/self-finance	%	51	51	51	51
Loans	%	49	49	49	49
Buildings, services					
Commercial					
Equity/self-finance	%	51	51	51	51
Bonds	%	6	6	6	6
Loans	%	33	33	33	33
Government					
Equity/self-finance	%	40	40	40	40
Bonds	%	30	30	30	30
Loans	%	30	30	30	30
Energy intensive industry					
Loan securitisation	%	10	20	20	20
Non-energy intensive industry					
Loan securitisation	%	10	20	20	20
Green cars					
Loan securitisation	%	10	30	30	30
Buildings, residential					
Loan securitisation	%	10	20	20	20
Buildings, services					
Loan securitisation	%	10	20	20	20

Table 3.A2.4. **Financial breakdown assumptions: Japan**

	Unit	2020	2025	2030	2035
Project finance					
Equity	%	18	18	18	18
Government	%	3.25	3	3	3
International financial institutions	%	9.75	10	10	10
Commercial loan	%	58	49	49	49
Bonds	%	7	10	10	10
Securitisation	%	4	10	10	10
Corporate finance					
Equity	%	14	14	14	14
Debt	%	86	86	86	86
Bonds	%	24	24	24	24
Long-term loans	%	62	62	62	62
Loan securitisation	%	10	10	10	10
Bond tenor	Years	15	15	15	15
Rooftop solar PV (financing model)					
Third-party ownership	%	30	0	0	0
Solar loan	%	70	0	0	0
Securitisation levels by type of finance					
Third-party securitisation	%	24	0	0	0
Loan securitisation	%	10	0	0	0
Government financing inputs					
Government leverage ratio in renewable energy	%	80	80	80	80
Government bond-to-loan ratio	%	80	80	80	80
Energy intensive industry					
Equity/self-finance	%	38	38	38	38
Bonds	%	5	5	5	5
Loans	%	47	47	47	47
Non-energy intensive industry					
Equity/self-finance	%	38	38	38	38
Bonds	%	5	5	5	5
Loans	%	47	47	47	47
Green cars					
Households					
Equity/self-finance	%	75	75	75	75
Loans	%	25	25	25	25
Leases	%	0	0	0	0
Commercial					
Equity/self-finance	%	89	89	89	89
Loans	%	11	11	11	11
Buildings, residential					
Households					
Equity/self-finance	%	51	51	51	51
Loans	%	49	49	49	49
Buildings, services					
Commercial					
Equity/self-finance	%	51	51	51	51
Bonds	%	6.37	6	6	6
Loans	%	32.63	33	33	33
Government					
Equity/self-finance	%	50	50	50	50
Bonds	%	50	50	50	50

Table 3.A2.4. **Financial breakdown assumptions: Japan** (*continued*)

	Unit	2020	2025	2030	2035
Loans	%	0	0	0	0
Energy intensive iIndustry					
Loan securitisation	%	6	10	10	10
Non-energy intensive industry					
Loan securitisation	%	6	10	10	10
Green cars					
Loan securitisation	%	6	10	10	10
Buildings, residential					
Loan securitisation	%	10	10	10	10
Buildings, services					
Loan securitisation	%	6	10	10	10

Annex 3.A3.
Model output by bond, geography and sector (baseline scenario)

Table 3.A3.1. **Model output of financing sources by geography and sector**

USD billion

Issuance		Japan				China (People's Republic of)				European Union				United States			
		2015-20	2021-25	2026-30	2031-35	2015-20	2021-25	2026-30	2031-35	2015-20	2021-25	2026-30	2031-35	2015-20	2021-25	2026-30	2031-35
Investment	Solar	7	7	6	12	13	16	14	17	11	11	20	15	9	19	13	13
	Wind	2	9	6	3	27	39	39	40	29	40	39	33	8	39	30	20
	Hydro	1	3	3	3	32	10	8	6	5	8	9	8	2	4	3	4
	Bio	1	1	1	3	4	8	13	10	4	5	9	38	7	11	8	8
	Cars	21	73	70	81	83	283	332	819	116	371	277	450	42	172	132	425
	Energy efficiency	14	18	22	25	33	42	55	66	61	75	86	92	42	53	67	72
	Total	**45**	**111**	**108**	**128**	**192**	**397**	**461**	**958**	**225**	**510**	**441**	**635**	**110**	**298**	**254**	**541**
Debt	Solar	6	6	5	9	10	12	11	13	8	8	15	11	7	15	10	10
	Wind	2	8	5	3	20	30	30	31	21	30	31	26	6	30	24	16
	Hydro	1	2	2	3	24	7	6	5	3	6	7	6	2	3	2	3
	Bio	1	1	1	3	3	6	9	7	3	4	7	28	5	8	6	6
	Cars	5	17	16	18	23	78	92	226	85	273	204	331	27	110	85	273
	Energy efficiency	7	9	12	13	18	23	31	37	31	38	43	46	21	27	35	37
	Total	**21**	**43**	**41**	**49**	**97**	**156**	**179**	**319**	**151**	**358**	**307**	**448**	**68**	**193**	**163**	**344**
Equity	Solar	1	1	1	2	3	4	3	4	3	3	5	3	2	5	3	3
	Wind	0	1	1	0	7	9	9	9	8	10	8	7	2	9	6	4
	Hydro	0	0	0	0	9	3	2	2	1	2	2	2	1	1	1	1
	Bio	0	0	0	1	1	2	3	2	1	1	2	10	2	3	2	2
	Cars	16	56	54	63	60	205	240	593	31	98	73	119	15	61	47	152
	Energy efficiency	7	9	11	12	15	18	24	29	31	37	43	46	20	26	32	36
	Total	**25**	**68**	**67**	**79**	**95**	**240**	**282**	**639**	**74**	**151**	**134**	**187**	**42**	**105**	**91**	**197**

Table 3.A3.1. **Model output of financing sources by geography and sector** (*continued*)

USD billion

Issuance		Japan				China (People's Republic of)				European Union				United States			
		2015-20	2021-25	2026-30	2031-35	2015-20	2021-25	2026-30	2031-35	2015-20	2021-25	2026-30	2031-35	2015-20	2021-25	2026-30	2031-35
Loans	Solar	4	4	3	6	7	8	7	8	5	4	7	5	3	6	4	3
	Wind	1	5	3	2	12	15	14	14	12	17	17	15	3	15	12	9
	Hydro	0	1	2	2	13	4	3	2	2	3	3	2	1	1	1	1
	Bio	1	1	1	2	1	3	4	3	2	2	3	9	3	3	2	2
	Cars	4	15	14	17	21	55	64	158	72	218	163	265	18	72	55	177
	Energy efficiency	4	5	7	7	12	14	19	23	16	20	22	23	9	11	15	15
	Total	**15**	**31**	**30**	**35**	**66**	**99**	**111**	**207**	**109**	**263**	**215**	**319**	**37**	**108**	**89**	**207**
Green bonds	Solar	2	2	2	3	3	4	4	5	3	4	8	7	3	9	6	7
	Wind	1	3	2	1	9	14	16	17	9	13	14	11	3	15	12	8
	Hydro	0	1	1	1	11	4	4	3	1	3	4	4	1	2	1	2
	Bio	0	0	0	1	1	3	5	4	1	2	4	19	2	5	4	4
	Cars	0	2	2	2	2	23	27	68	13	55	41	66	9	39	30	95
	Energy efficiency	3	4	5	5	6	9	11	15	14	18	21	23	12	16	20	21
	Total	**6**	**12**	**11**	**14**	**32**	**57**	**68**	**112**	**42**	**95**	**92**	**129**	**31**	**85**	**74**	**137**
Total finance		**45**	**111**	**108**	**128**	**192**	**397**	**461**	**958**	**225**	**510**	**441**	**635**	**110**	**298**	**254**	**541**
Green bonds type	Municipal/ sovereign	2	3	4	4	2	2	3	4	7	9	11	11	6	9	9	10
	IFI	1	1	1	2	4	5	6	7	3	4	6	7	1	3	3	3
	Corporate	1	3	2	2	11	10	10	10	11	14	15	17	9	19	16	13
	Project bond	0	1	1	1	10	10	12	13	1	2	4	10	0	2	2	3
	Asset-backed securities	1	4	4	5	5	31	37	78	20	66	56	84	15	52	43	108
	Total	**6**	**12**	**11**	**14**	**32**	**57**	**68**	**112**	**42**	**95**	**92**	**129**	**31**	**85**	**74**	**137**
Secondary green bond issuance		4	9	9	11	20	30	33	62	33	79	64	96	11	32	27	62
Total green bonds		**10**	**21**	**20**	**24**	**51**	**87**	**101**	**174**	**75**	**174**	**156**	**225**	**42**	**117**	**101**	**199**

IFI: international financial institution.

Table 3.A3.2. **Model output of bond issuance by geography and sector**

USD billion

Amount outstanding		Japan					China (People's Republic of)					European Union					United States					4 regions				
		2015	2020	2025	2030	2035	2015	2020	2025	2030	2035	2015	2020	2025	2030	2035	2015	2020	2025	2030	2035	2015	2020	2025	2030	2035
Photovoltaic	Municipal/ sovereign	1	3	7	9	11	0	1	3	6	9	1	6	10	18	19	1	6	15	21	23	3	16	35	53	62
	IFI	0	1	2	2	3	0	1	3	5	6	0	1	3	5	6	0	1	2	4	4	1	4	10	16	20
	Corporate	1	3	6	8	8	1	5	11	14	13	1	7	13	21	20	1	8	20	26	27	4	24	50	69	69
	Project bond	0	0	1	2	3	0	4	10	17	21	0	0	2	6	12	0	0	2	6	10	0	5	15	30	46
	Asset-backed securities	1	3	6	9	11	0	2	7	13	18	1	6	13	26	33	1	6	23	35	43	3	18	50	83	104
Wind	Municipal/ sovereign	0	0	2	2	3	0	2	5	9	12	1	5	11	16	17	0	1	7	12	14	1	9	25	39	46
	IFI	0	0	2	3	4	1	5	12	20	25	1	5	13	20	23	0	1	7	11	14	2	12	34	54	66
	Corporate	0	2	7	10	11	3	19	39	54	55	5	31	64	88	84	2	11	52	79	86	11	63	163	232	236
	Project bond	0	0	1	2	2	0	14	39	72	96	0	1	4	7	9	0	0	3	6	8	0	16	46	87	116
	Asset-backed securities	0	1	4	6	7	0	3	14	28	41	1	8	25	45	55	0	2	22	43	54	2	14	65	122	157
Energy efficiency	Municipal/ sovereign	2	10	22	34	42	1	5	10	15	19	5	31	63	94	108	4	26	53	83	99	12	72	148	227	268
	IFI	0	3	6	9	11	2	10	21	34	49	1	9	19	31	38	1	4	8	13	16	4	25	54	87	115
	Corporate	0	2	3	5	7	2	12	24	34	45	3	16	35	54	65	4	22	46	71	85	9	51	108	165	200
	Project bond																					0	0	0	0	0
	Asset-backed securities	1	3	11	13	15	4	17	115	145	315	18	81	271	224	333	13	60	196	168	439	35	161	594	549	1 101
Bioenergy	Municipal/ sovereign	0	0	0	0	1	0	2	3	3	2	0	0	1	1	2	0	0	0	0	1	0	3	4	6	5
	IFI	0	0	1	1	2	1	7	9	10	6	0	1	3	4	6	0	0	1	1	2	1	8	13	17	15
	Corporate	0	1	3	4	5	4	25	30	31	13	1	6	13	19	20	1	4	8	11	12	6	35	54	65	50
	Project bond	0	0	0	1	2	0	18	33	41	30	0	0	2	6	11	0	0	1	2	5	0	18	36	50	47
	Asset-backed securities	0	0	1	2	3	1	3	6	9	8	0	1	4	8	11	0	0	2	4	6	1	5	14	24	29

Table 3.A3.2. **Model output of bond issuance by geography and sector** (*continued*)

USD billion

Amount outstanding		Japan					China (People's Republic of)					European Union					United States					4 regions				
		2015	2020	2025	2030	2035	2015	2020	2025	2030	2035	2015	2020	2025	2030	2035	2015	2020	2025	2030	2035	2015	2020	2025	2030	2035
Hydro energy	Municipal/ sovereign	0	0	0	0	0	0	0	1	2	2	0	0	1	1	4	0	0	1	1	2	0	1	2	5	9
	IFI	0	0	0	1	1	0	1	2	5	7	0	1	2	4	13	0	1	3	4	5	0	3	7	14	26
	Corporate	0	1	2	2	3	0	3	7	13	16	1	5	10	17	40	2	11	23	30	29	3	19	42	63	88
	Project bond	0	0	0	1	1	0	2	7	15	24	0	0	1	5	25	0	0	3	6	11	0	3	11	27	61
	Asset-backed securities	0	0	1	1	2	0	0	3	7	11	0	1	3	7	27	0	1	6	11	15	1	3	12	27	55
Total	Municipal/ sovereign	2	14	30	46	57	2	11	22	35	44	7	42	85	131	151	6	33	77	118	139	17	100	215	330	390
	SSA	1	4	10	17	22	4	24	48	74	93	3	17	39	64	86	1	7	21	33	41	9	53	118	188	241
	Corporate	1	8	21	30	34	11	64	111	147	142	11	65	135	199	229	9	55	150	218	238	32	193	417	594	643
	Project bonds	0	1	3	5	8	0	38	89	145	171	0	2	9	24	57	0	1	8	20	34	0	42	108	194	270
	Asset-backed securities and CLO	1	8	24	31	39	5	26	145	201	392	20	97	316	311	459	15	71	250	261	557	42	201	735	805	1 447
Secondary issuance (FI)	Seconday issuance	4	26	65	88	101	20	118	237	323	473	33	197	512	606	728	11	66	204	261	439	74	447	1 157	1 450	2 078
Total outstanding																						**174**	**1 035**	**2 750**	**3 560**	**5 069**

Notes: IFI: international financial institution ; SSA: supranational, sub-sovereign and agency; CLO: collateralised loan obligation.

Annex 3.A4. Annotations for Figure 3.23

Direct unlisted investments in projects

Direct unlisted project debt

The Westmill Solar Cooperative refinanced its 5 MW Watchfield solar PV plant in Oxfordshire with a GBP 12 million bond privately placed with UK Lancashire County Pension Fund.

Intermediated unlisted investments in projects

Intermediated unlisted project debt

No public information available regarding institutional investment in an unlisted green project bond fund.

Intermediated listed project investment

Intermediated listed project debt

The Nordic Investment Bank (NIB) issued a five-year SEK 1 billion NIB Environment Bond (NEB), the third and largest Swedish krona-denominated bond at the time of issuance in April 2015 (Nordic Investment Bank, 2015). Swedish pension fund Storebrand and Danish pension fund PKA invested in the issuance (Nordic Investment Bank, 2015).

The African Development Bank issued a five-year SEK 1 billion fixed-rate green bond in March 2014. The transaction was placed with 16 investors including AP2, AP3, Landstinget Västmanland, SAAB Pensionsstiftelse, SEB Fonder, SPP/Storebrand, Svenska Kyrkan and Systembolaget AB (AfDB, 2014).

The Asian Development Bank (ADB) raised USD 500 million in its inaugural green bond issuance in March 2015. The ten-year 2.2% coupon bonds will fund ADB projects that promote low-carbon and climate-resilient development in Asia (ADB, 2015). The bonds were sold to 44 investors including: AP2, AP3, AP4, Baloise Insurance, Banque Syz & Co SA, Blackrock, Calvert Investments, Donner & Reuschel Asset Management, Mirova, Nikko Asset Management Europe Ltd, Nippon Life Insurance Company, Omega Global Investors on behalf of Local Government Super, Praxis Intermediate Income Fund, SEB Wealth, State Street Global Advisors, and TIAA-CREF (ADB, 2015).

Bank of America Corporation issued a three-year, fixed-rate USD 500 million green bond in November 2013. Proceeds will be used to finance green investments such as renewable energy and energy efficiency projects. Bank of America viewed this issuance as an opportunity to expand its investor base and participating investors include the following: AP4, BlackRock, Breckinridge Capital Advisors, California State Teachers' Retirement System, Calvert Investment Management, Pax World Management LLC, Praxis Intermediate Income Fund, State Street Global Advisors, Standish Mellon Asset Management Company LLC, TIAA-CREF, Trillium Asset Management, LLC (Bank of America, 2013).

The World Bank issued a EUR 30 million 30-year fixed rate green bond in February 2015 to fund projects that meet low-carbon and climate-resilient criteria (World Bank, 2015). The World Bank issued the bond in response to demand for longer maturities from Zurich Insurance Group and as a 30-year bond it is the longest maturity fixed-rate green bond issued by the World Bank to date (World Bank, 2015).

In 2010, Nikko Asset Management launched two green bond funds, one targeted at Japanese investors and another for international investors, that would invest 100% of its portfolio in World Bank-issued green bonds in 2010 (World Bank, 2010a). The World Bank issued ten new green bonds for the fund launch denominated in ten different currencies including Australian dollars, Colombian pesos, Russian roubles, Turkish lira and South African rand (World Bank, 2010b). In the two years after the fund launch, Nikko Investment Management raised more than USD 500 million from Japanese retail investors and USD 40 million from European and US institutional investors. Notable investors include Silicon Valley Community Foundation and Truestone Impact Investment Management (World Bank, 2012).

A diverse pool of institutional investors has purchased green bonds issued by the World Bank to fund diverse projects that support climate change adaptation or mitigation. Since 2008, the World Bank has issued approximately USD 4 billion in green bonds (World Bank, 2013). Notable pension fund investors include Sweden's AP Fonden 2 and AP Fonden 3, CalSTRS, New York Common Retirement Fund, and the UN Joint Staff Pension Fund (World Bank, 2013).

The World Bank issued its first AUD-denominated Kangaroo Bond in 2014. Australian superannuation fund UniSuper was the cornerstone investor for the issuance, purchasing AUD 100 million of the total AUD 300 million offering (Fernyhough, 2014).

Direct (in-house) listed project investments

A listed green project bond can provide financing for a single project, a portfolio of similar or standardised projects (such as wind farms or rooftop solar panel installations), or a portfolio of diverse sustainable energy infrastructure projects.

Solar Star Funding, LLC, a wholly-owned subsidiary of MidAmerican Energy Holdings Co., issued a USD 1 billion project bond in 2013 linked to the 580 MW Solar Star PV project which at the time of the issuance was the largest renewable project bond ever issued (BNEF, 2014). US pension fund CalSTRS invested in the issuance (CalSTRS, 2014).

SolarCity issued a 4.80% USD 54.4 million solar-backed asset-backed security in November 2013. The underlying assets are 44 MW of solar PV across 5 033 projects in the United States, 71% residential (BNEF, 2014). Investors in the issuance included Aviva, Blackrock, Angel Oak Capital Advisors, Transamerica Life, and Accordia Life and Ann (BNEF, 2014).

Toyota Financial Services, the financial services arm of the Japanese automaker Toyota, issued a USD 1.75 billion green bond in March 2014. The bond was the first auto industry asset-backed (ABS) green bond. Proceeds will be used to fund new retail finance contracts and lease contracts for Toyota and Lexus vehicles that meet specific green criteria related to emissions and fuels efficiency (Toyota Financial Services, 2014). The green bonds are a standard auto loan-backed ABS where cash flow is linked to repayments of outstanding loans for the company's cars. Asset managers and pension funds investing in the issuance included TIAA-CREF, Vanguard Group, Northern Trust, SEI Investments and CalSTRS (BNEF, 2014; CalSTRS 2014).

The Soitec project bond was issued to finance the Touwsrivier solar power plant using concentrated photovoltaic technology. The South African bond was issued in local currency and attracted a diverse pool of investors, including South African pension funds and asset managers (Soitec, 2013).

A publically listed solar project finance bond was issued by Solar Power Generation Ltd to fund two 5 MW solar PV plants in England. The UK Pension Insurance Corporation purchased the entire GBP 40 million offering (Pension Insurance Corporation, 2012).

Direct unlisted investments in pure-play corporates

Direct unlisted (private) corporate debt

No public information available on institutional investment in a privately placed corporate green bond.

Intermediated unlisted pure-play corporate investment

Intermediated unlisted debt provision for pure-play companies

No public information available regarding institutional investment in an unlisted corporate green bond fund.

Intermediated listed pure-play corporate investment

Listed pure-play corporate debt

Export Development Canada issued its inaugural USD 300 million green bond in 2014, and its second USD 300 million green bond in 2015, to fund loans to companies active in preservation, protection or remediation of air, water and/or soil; creation of renewable energy; and mitigation of climate change (EDC, 2014; 2015). Californian pension fund CalSTRS invested in the issuance (CalSTRS, 2014; 2016).

Direct (in-house) listed corporate pure-play investment

Direct (in-house) corporate pure-play listed debt

In November 2013, EDF issued a EUR 1.4 billion green bond with proceeds used to finance the development or construction costs associated with new renewable energy projects developed by EDF Energies Nouvelles (EDF, 2014). Asset manager Jupiter Fund Management invested in the issuance (Kelly, 2013) and as of December 2014 the funds contributed to the financing of 13 renewable energy projects (wind, solar PV, biogas) in Canada, France and the United States (EDF, 2014).

PNE Wind AG, a German wind farm project developer, issued a EUR 100 million 8% corporate bond to expand offshore and onshore wind activities. Institutional investors invested EUR 33.7 million in the issuance (PNE Wind, 2013).

References

ADB (2015), "Inaugural ADB green bond to drive more funds to climate change projects", news release, 13 March, Asian Development Bank, www.adb.org/news/inaugural-adb-green-bond-drive-more-funds-climate-change-projects.

AfDB (2014), "AfDB prices SEK 1 billion green bond due March 2019", press release, 10 March, African Development Bank, www.afdb.org/en/news-and-events/article/afdb-prices-sek-1-billion-green-bond-due-march-2019-12887.

Bank of America (2013), "Bank of America issues $500 million 'green bond'", press release, 21 November, Bank of America, http://newsroom.bankofamerica.com/press-releases/corporate-and-financial-news/bank-america-issues-500-million-green-bond.

BNEF (2014), "Green bonds market outlook 2014: Blooming with new varietals", 2 June, Bloomberg Finance L.P., http://about.bnef.com/white-papers/green-bonds-market-outlook-2014/content/uploads/sites/4/2014/06/2014-06-02-Green-bonds-market-outlook-2014.pdf.

CalSTRS (2016), "Green Initiative Task Force: 2016 annual report", California State Teachers' Retirement System, West Sacramento, California, www.calstrs.com/sites/main/files/file-attachments/green_report_2016.pdf.

CalSTRS (2014), "Green Initiative Task Force: 2014 annual report", California State Teachers' Retirement System, West Sacramento, California, www.calstrs.com/sites/main/files/file-attachments/green_initiative_task_force_2014_annual_report.pdf.

EDC (2015), "EDC responds to demand for sustainable investment with new green bond", News Release, 1 December, Export Development Canada, www.edc.ca/EN/About-Us/News-Room/News-Releases/Pages/green-bond-2015.aspx.

EDC (2014), "Export Development Canada issues first green bond", News Release, 23 January, Export Development Canada.

EDF (2014), "Reference document: Annual financial report 2014", Électricité de France, Paris, www.edf.fr/sites/default/files/contrib/finance/document-de-reference/EDF_DDR_2014_VA.pdf.

Fernyhough, J. (2014), "World Bank issues kangaroo green bond", *Financial Standard*, 17 April, https://www.financialstandard.com.au/news/world-bank-issues-kangaroo-green-bond-39544597.

Kelly, J. (2013), "New buyers show growing taste for 'green bonds'", Reuters, 2 December, http://uk.reuters.com/article/2013/12/02/uk-green-bonds-idUKBRE9B104E20131202.

Nordic Investment Bank (2015), "SEK 1 billion 5-year NIB Environmental Bond (NEB)", joint press release, 17 April, Nordic Investment Bank, https://www.nib.int/filebank/a/1429277635/ed6efb5c76ab0a2c0df8e16d90cf400b/4421-JPR_2015_NEB_SEK_1bn.pdf.

Pension Insurance Corporation (2012), "Pension Insurance Corporation invests GBP 40 million in solar plant", press release, 22 November, https://www.pensioncorporation.com/media/31330/pension-insurance-corporation-invests-40m-in-solar-plant.pdf.

PNE Wind (2013), "Explanation of the top-up of the Corporate Bond", corporate news, 16 September, www.pnewind.com/investor-relations/ir-news/corporate-news/artikel/explanation-to-the-top-up-of-the-corporate-bond.

Soitec (2013), "Soitec Completes ZAR 1,000,000,000 inaugural solar financing bond transaction in South Africa", press release, 30 April.

Toyota Financial Services (2014), "Prospectus supplement to prospectus dated March 5, 2014", Toyota Motor Credit Corporation, 11 March, https://www.sc.toyotafinancial.com/web/tfs/pub/contents/investorRelations/TAOT%202014-A%20Final%20Prospectus.PDF.

World Bank (2015), "World Bank issues EUR 30 million fixed rate green bond due 2045", press release, 17 February, The World Bank, http://treasury.worldbank.org/cmd/htm/EUR_30million_GreenBond.html.

World Bank (2013), "Green bond fact sheet", The World Bank Treasury, Washington, DC, March, http://treasury.worldbank.org/cmd/WorldBankGreenBondFactSheet.pdf.

World Bank (2012), "Green bond: Fourth annual investor update 2012", The World Bank Treasury, Washington, DC, http://treasury.worldbank.org/cmd/pdf/WorldBankGreenBondNewsletter2012.pdf.

World Bank (2010a), "Nikko Asset Management set to launch green fund with World Bank Bonds", press release, 22 February, The World Bank, http://treasury.worldbank.org/cmd/htm/NikkoAM_WB_GreenBond.html.

World Bank (2010b), "World Bank announces ten new green bonds denominated in ten different currencies", press release, 23 February, The World Bank, http://treasury.worldbank.org/cmd/htm/USDeq355millionGreenBonds.html.

Glossary

450 Scenario: A scenario presented in the International Energy Agency's (IEA) *World Energy Outlook* that sets out an energy pathway consistent with the goal of limiting the global increase in temperature to 2°C by limiting concentration of greenhouse gases in the atmosphere to around 450 parts per million of CO_2.

Asset-backed security (ABS): A financial security backed by a loan, lease or receivables against assets other than real estate and mortgages.

Asset and liability management: The task of managing the funds of a financial institution to accomplish two goals: 1) to earn an adequate return on funds invested; and 2) to maintain a comfortable surplus of assets beyond liabilities.

Asset liability matching: Process of managing, investing, purchasing and selling activities to ensure that cash is available for meeting the obligations as they fall due.

Bankable: Projects that have sufficient collateral, probability of success and predictability of future cash flow, to be acceptable to prospective financiers.

Benchmark: The performance of a pre-determined set of securities, used for comparison purposes. Such sets may be based on published indexes or may be customised to suit an investment strategy.

Break-even level: A level at which the volume of sales or revenues exactly equals total expenses, therefore there is neither a profit or a loss.

Capital recycling: Providing refinancing once a project is at the operational stage so that early-stage investors have an "exit strategy", allowing them to free up capital to invest in new projects – i.e. to "recycle" their capital.

Co-investment: A form of direct investing whereby institutional investors partner up with other investors to invest in an asset.

Corporate bond: Debt obligations issued by corporations.

Cost of capital: The cost of funds used for financing a business. Cost of capital depends on the mode of financing used – it refers to the cost of equity if the business is financed solely through equity, or to the cost of debt if it is financed solely through debt. Many companies use a combination of debt and equity to finance their businesses, and for such companies, their overall cost of capital is derived from a weighted average of all capital sources, widely known as the weighted average cost of capital (WACC). Since the cost of capital represents a hurdle rate that a company must overcome before it can generate value, it is extensively used in the capital budgeting process to determine whether the company should proceed with a project.

Coupon: The contractual interest obligation a bond or debenture issuer covenants to pay to its debtholders.

Covered bonds: Debt securities backed by cash flows from mortgages or public sector loans. Covered bonds employ a "dual recourse structure" where bond investors have a claim over: 1) a "cover pool" of assets, the quality of which is strictly regulated; and 2) a general unsecured claim against the issuer. This dual recourse structure enables covered bonds to enjoy superior credit ratings and lower funding costs compared with unsecured debt issued by banks. At the same time, because of strict oversight for what can go into the "cover pool", they generally carry less risk than pure asset-backed securities.

Credit enhancement: Reducing the credit or default risk of a debt, thereby improving its credit-worthiness and increasing the overall credit rating.

Credit rating: Credit rating refers to an evaluation of individual's or company's ability to repay obligations or its likelihood of not defaulting. If a credit rating is downgraded, it would increase the cost of capital due to the extent that the reward for such risky assets would be necessary as risk premium.

Deleveraging: The reduction of the ratio of debt in the balance sheet of an economic entity. In this report, deleveraging refers to the attempt to decrease the financial leverage ratio (value of a firm's debt to the total value of the firm). Banks have been lowering their high pre-crisis leverage levels and are preparing for stricter regulatory capital requirements, and in the process have been reducing their lending.

Diversification: Dividing investment funds among a variety of securities with different risk, reward and correlation statistics so as to minimise unsystematic risk.

Feed-in tariff: A fixed price per kWh of electricity which is paid to the producer by the system operator.

Feed-in premium (FiP): A premium which is paid to the producer on top of the electricity market price.

Financing instrument: A financing instrument is a tradable asset of any kind; either cash, evidence of an ownership interest in an entity, or a contractual right to receive or deliver cash or another financing instrument.

Fund: An investment company that invests the funds which are aggregated and pooled from individual investors for a fee. An investment fund gives individual investors access to a wider range of financial products than investors themselves would have been able to access.

Green investment bank: Broadly defined as a public entity established specifically to facilitate and "crowd-in" domestic private low-carbon climate-resilient infrastructure investments through different activities and interventions.

Grid-parity: Grid parity refers to an energy source that can generate electricity at a levelised cost that is less than or equal to the price of purchasing power from the electricity grid.

Headline risk: The risk that a major event or story will spread throughout the media and will negatively impact a company's stock price or reputation.

Illiquid: In the context of investments the term illiquid describes a thinly traded investment such as a stock or bond that is not easily converted into cash. Illiquid securities have higher transactions costs.

Infrastructure fund: Investment fund that is established to invest in infrastructure assets.

Institutional investor: Institutional investors are usually synonymous with "intermediary investors", that is to say, an institution that manages and invests other people's money. The term institutional investor can be used to describe insurance companies, investment funds, pension funds, public pension reserve funds (social security systems), foundations and endowments, among others.

Investment bank: An investment bank traditionally facilitates transactions of all types in the wholesale financial markets (transactions conducted by corporations, businesses, institutional investors and high net-worth individuals), including mergers and acquisitions (the purchase and sale of businesses and their assets), capital raising or "underwriting" (of equity, bonds, etc.) on behalf of corporations or their shareholders. They may provide ancillary services such as market making, trading of derivatives, securities and other financial instruments, investing and lending, asset management and FICC services (fixed-income instruments, currencies and commodities). This excludes retail brokerage, retail lending or any other practice that centres on "unaccredited investors".

Investment grade: In the context of bond ratings, the rating level above which institutional investors have been authorised to invest. Investment-grade bonds are those that are assigned a rating in the top four categories by commercial credit rating companies. S&P classifies investment-grade bonds as BBB or higher, and Moody's classifies investment-grade bonds as BAA or higher.

Leverage: The use of debt financing at a proportionally greater amount than comparable investments.

Liquidity: In the context of a corporation, the ability of the corporation to meet its short-term obligations. In the context of securities, a high level of trading activity, allowing buying and selling with minimum price disturbance. Also, a market characterised by the ability to buy and sell with relative ease.

Long-dated liabilities: A section of the balance sheet that lists obligations of the company that become due more than one year into the future.

Mark to market: The practice of valuing an asset or a liability using current market prices. "Mark to market" is referred to as "fair value accounting" and is the practice of updating the value of an asset or a liability to reflect its real market value rather than the initial cost of the asset or liability.

Maturity transformation: The process of converting short-term sources of finance (e.g. deposits from retail savers) into long-term borrowings (e.g. loans, mortgages, etc.).

Monoline insurer: Monoline insurers are financial institutions focused solely on insuring bond issuers such as municipal governments against default. Bond issuers buy this insurance to upgrade the credit-worthiness of their bonds, making the overall cost lower by giving confidence that the insured security would be paid in full. The first monolines were set up in the United States in the 1970s, covering municipal and corporate bond issues. These insurers suffered when the financial crisis hit, as some lacked sufficient capital to cover their liabilities adequately. Several had their credit ratings reduced, effectively downgrading them to junk status.

New Policies Scenario: A scenario in the IEA's *World Energy Outlook* that takes account of broad policy commitments and plans that have been announced by countries, including national pledges to reduce greenhouse gas emissions and plans to phase out fossil energy subsidies, even if the measures to implement these commitments have yet to be identified or announced. This broadly serves as the IEA's baseline scenario.

Private placement debt: A type of debt that is generated when a bond or some other type of security is sold directly to a limited number of investors in a non-public offering.

Project bond: Private debt issued by a project company to finance a specific off-balance sheet project. Project bonds are an asset-based form of financing.

Public finance institutions: Publicly created or mandated financial institutions that have often been created to correct for the lack of market-based finance through the provision of missing financial services.

Pure-play: In financial management, "pure-play" entities are focused on only one industry or product.

Ring-fencing: Practice of financially separating a portion of a company's assets or profits without necessarily being operated as a separate unit. Ring-fencing may occur for regulatory, financing or taxation purposes.

Risk-adjusted return: A measure of valuing return on investment calculated in a way that takes into account the risks associated with the investment. Being able to compare a high-risk, potentially high-return investment with a low-risk, lower return investment helps to answer a key question that confronts every investor: is it worth the risk? There are several ways to calculate risk-adjusted return. Each has its strengths and shortcomings. All require particular data, such as an investment's rate of return, the risk-free return rate for a given period, and a market's performance and its standard deviation. Risk-adjusted returns can apply to individual securities and investment funds and portfolios.

Risk mitigant: A targeted financial intervention that is aimed at reducing, reassigning or re-apportioning different investment risks.

Risk profile: An assessment of the degree to which an investor is prepared to accept losses at the expense of potential gain.

Securitisation: The process of transforming illiquid financial assets into tradable products.

Special-purpose vehicle: Legal entity created to fulfil a specific and well-defined financial or regulatory objectives. For project finance, a special-purpose vehicle may be created to hold the assets associated with a project therefore keeping the investment off the balance sheets of project developers. Within the securitisation framework, a special-purpose vehicle can be a legal entity which may issue securities or other debt instruments, may legally or economically own assets underlying the issue of the securities mentioned above, and be financially and legally isolated from the originator.

Term loan: Loan payable in a fixed number of equal instalments over the term of the loan. Term loans are generally short term (between one and five years) and are usually provided as working capital for acquiring income-producing assets (machinery, equipment, inventory, etc.) that generate cash flows to repay the loan.

Transaction enabler: A process or technique which facilitates investment by reducing the associated transaction costs or otherwise enabling the investment to be made.

Underwriting: In the case of loans, underwriting is the process by which a lender decides whether a potential creditor is creditworthy and should receive a loan. For securities issuances, underwriting is the procedure by which an underwriter, such as an investment bank, brings a new security issue to the investing public in an offering. In such a case, the underwriter will guarantee a certain price for a certain number of securities to the party that is issuing the security (in exchange for a fee). Thus, the issuer is secure that they will raise a certain minimum from the issue, while the underwriter bears the risk of the issue.

YieldCo: A publicly traded company that is formed to own operating assets that produce cash flows. The cash is distributed to investors as dividends.

Note: Explanations of the terms are very condensed and may not be complete. They are not considered to necessarily reflect the official position of the OECD. Sources used include, among others, Duke University's Hypertextual Finance Glossary; Brealey, Myers and Allen (2014); and Investopedia.com.

ORGANISATION FOR ECONOMIC CO-OPERATION AND DEVELOPMENT

The OECD is a unique forum where governments work together to address the economic, social and environmental challenges of globalisation. The OECD is also at the forefront of efforts to understand and to help governments respond to new developments and concerns, such as corporate governance, the information economy and the challenges of an ageing population. The Organisation provides a setting where governments can compare policy experiences, seek answers to common problems, identify good practice and work to co-ordinate domestic and international policies.

The OECD member countries are: Australia, Austria, Belgium, Canada, Chile, the Czech Republic, Denmark, Estonia, Finland, France, Germany, Greece, Hungary, Iceland, Ireland, Israel, Italy, Japan, Korea, Latvia, Luxembourg, Mexico, the Netherlands, New Zealand, Norway, Poland, Portugal, the Slovak Republic, Slovenia, Spain, Sweden, Switzerland, Turkey, the United Kingdom and the United States. The European Union takes part in the work of the OECD.

OECD Publishing disseminates widely the results of the Organisation's statistics gathering and research on economic, social and environmental issues, as well as the conventions, guidelines and standards agreed by its members.

OECD PUBLISHING, 2, rue André-Pascal, 75775 PARIS CEDEX 16
(97 2017 05 1 P) ISBN 978-92-64-27231-6 – 2017

www.ingramcontent.com/pod-product-compliance
Ingram Content Group UK Ltd.
Pitfield, Milton Keynes, MK11 3LW, UK
UKHW051505290926
15471UKWH00008B/1440

9 789264 272316